DEAD TOWNS
OF ALABAMA

Centennial Celebration at St. Stephens, Alabama, May 6, 1899, showing the U.S. Revenue Cutter *Winona* and the river steamer *Minnie Lee*
unloading guests at the abandoned site. (Courtesy Alabama State
Department of Archives and History.)

DEAD
TOWNS
OF ALABAMA

W. STUART HARRIS

THE UNIVERSITY OF ALABAMA PRESS
Tuscaloosa

Originally published in honor of the American Revolution Bicentennial,
1776–1976

First Paperbound Printing 2001

Map copyright © 2001

9 8 7 6 5 4 3 2 1
10 09 08 07 06 05 04 03 02 01

∞

The paper on which this book is printed meets the minimum require-
ments of American National Standard for Information Science-Perma-
nence of Paper for Printed Library Materials, ANSI Z39.48-1984.

Cover design by Robin McDonald

Typepface: New Baskerville

Library of Congress Cataloging-in-Publication Data

Harris, W. Stuart, 1933–
    Dead towns of Alabama
    Bibliography: p.
    Includes index.
    1. Alabama—Antiquities. 2. Cities and towns, Extinct,
ruined, etc.—Alabama. 3. Indians of North America—Alabama—Antiq-
uites. 4. Fortification—Alabama. I. Title.
F338.H37976.176–29655
ISBN 0-8173-1125-4
ISBN 978-0-8173-1125-4

Dedicated to my wife Barbara, who has encouraged my interest in Alabama history, and to my children, Lee, Bill, Cathy, and Jenny, who have
often accompanied me in my ventures to the dead towns of the state.

CONTENTS

Counties of Alabama

PREFACE

Today many people have developed an interest in reading about and visiting dead towns, or, as some prefer to call them, ghost towns. A dead town is a place where people once lived and conducted business, where homes and other buildings once existed, but which are now empty, lifeless, and all but forgotten. Such sites formerly appeared on maps and in atlases, but are now omitted. A few years ago only professional historians were interested in these forgotten sites. Now students, history buffs, and families on outings enjoy exploring areas far from the beaten paths, across plowed fields, or through briar-infested wilderness areas, searching for reminders of another time. It is for those interested in dead towns that I have compiled this book. I have classified the sites into three sections: Indian towns and villages; fort sites; and colonial, territorial, and state dead towns.

Alabama is rich in historical lore. Indians made the area their home for possibly as long as 10,000 years. Spanish sailors visited the coastal area in 1519, and Hernando DeSoto transversed much of the state in 1540. The first true colony was established by the French in 1702, and trading forts were soon erected in the wilderness. Pioneers built homes in the wilderness, and their descendents reaped the harvest of their labors. Alabama has had five capitals, two of which have become dead towns.

Very few dead town studies have been published. The first full-length monograph on dead towns was written in 1878 by the prominent Georgia historian, Charles Colcock Jones, Jr. Entitled *The Dead Towns of Georgia*, this classic described a number of towns, such as Old Ebenezer, Frederica, Hardwicke, and Sunbury, which flourished in the early days of Georgia's history. Im-

portant historically, these studies made fascinating reading for
the novice as well as for the professional historian. Jones later
referred to many of these towns in his two-volume *History of
Georgia,* published in 1883.

In recent years, the study of dead towns has centered on states
in the western section of the country. In *Ghosts of the Glory Trail*
(1956), Nell Murbarger listed 275 ghost towns in the old mining
areas of eastern California, Nevada, and Utah. The Work Projects Administration compiled information of a similar nature in
Ghost Towns of Colorado (1947). Michael Jenkinson in *Ghost Towns
of New Mexico* (1967) listed historical information along with many
photographs of the remains of the abandoned towns of the past.
Two states have published maps of their dead towns as a means
of attracting tourists. The map prepared by the Montana Highway Commission lists 93 ghost towns, while several hundred
ghost towns, trading posts, and abandoned stagecoach and rail
stops appear on Lucien A. File's "Ghost Town Map of New Mexico" (1964), distributed by the New Mexico Department of
Development.

No full-length study of Alabama dead towns has been published, although William H. Jenkins, former president of the
Alabama Historical Association, presented a listing of some of
the towns at the annual meeting of the Association in April, 1958,
since published in *The Alabama Review,* XII (October, 1959), 281–
85. Often information concerning dead towns can be found in
monographs pertaining to place names. William Alexander
Read's *Indian Place-Names in Alabama* (1934) and Virginia Oden
Foscue's *Sumter County Place-Names* (1959), a master's thesis at the
University of Alabama, are excellent examples of this type of research. More studies of this nature are needed.

This volume should not be construed to be a definitive work
on all the dead towns of Alabama, even though it contains the
sites and brief histories of 83 Indian towns, 47 fort sites, and 112
colonial, territorial, or state towns of the historic period. The
author has found definitization to be virtually an impossible task
concerning Alabama, a state with such a long and varied history.

As to the locations listed in this volume, it must be remembered
that they are only approximate, because some sites, such as that

of Maubila, are debatable or shrouded in mystery; most of the
locations, however, are accurate. These sites are often on private
property, so permission to visit them must first be obtained, or
trespassing charges may be filed by angry property owners. One
cannot blame such an owner when one sees the results of wanton
destruction at historical sites.

Careless digging on historical sites by "pot hunters" (a derog-
atory term used to describe persons interested only in making
additions to their own private collections of artifacts and not in
proper research methods) is not only a sure way to destroy evidences of the past, but also may be a violation of federal or state
laws. The Antiquities Act of 1906 protects all federal lands from
such encroachment; permission to excavate may be granted to
reputable societies or institutions provided that proper records
are kept and that all recoveries are deposited in public reposi-
tories or museums. Archaeological "diggings" on state lands in
Alabama are under the confines of the Alabama Geological Survey, and amateur archaeological research is unlawful unless
proper permission to excavate is granted by that department.
Anyone sincerely interested in archaeological research should
become involved in the activities of such organizations as the Alabama Archaeological Society, or may enroll in many programs
of that nature at various colleges and universities.

Under no circumstances should a person destroy evidences
of our heritage through careless enthusiasm, but should channel
this energy through a proper education in the subject field. Be-
sides courses offered by our educational institutions in archaeology, many excellent volumes have been published pertaining
to this interesting area. Emma Lila Fundaburk and Mary Doug-
lass Foreman's *Sun Circles and Human Hands*, published in 1957,
is perhaps the most definitive volume on Indian artifacts, es-
pecially in Alabama and the Southeastern states. Fundaburk's
Southeastern Indians, Life Portraits and Thomas M. N. Lewis' and
Madeline Kneberg's *Tribes That Slumber* are also indispensable in
this type of regional study. A vast number of books have been
published pertaining to archaeological research methods, such
as *The Amateur Archaeologist's Handbook*, by Maurice Robbins and
Mary B. Irving (1965), and *Hidden America*, by Roland Wells

Robbins and Evan Jones (1959), which is mainly concerned with archaeology and the historical period. In regard to the excavations of fort sites, perhaps Jean Carl Harrington's *Search For The Cittie of Ralegh, Archaeological Excavations At Fort Raleigh National Historic Site, North Carolina,* published by the National Park Service in 1962, would be enlightening. For a thorough study of artifacts found in trash pits in the vicinity of the ruins of a colonial mansion, the author would suggest the reading of Ivor Noel Hume's *Excavations At Rosewell, Gloucester County, Virginia, 1957–1959,* published by the Smithsonian Institution in 1962.

The Smith Home, situated near Elyton, remained a Birmingham landmark until it was recently razed.

DEAD TOWNS
OF ALABAMA

PART I

INDIAN TOWNS
AND VILLAGES

Although people have lived in Alabama for nearly 10,000 years, this study lists the known sites of the historic period rather than the hundreds of mounds and evidences of habitation from the prehistoric era. Indian towns and villages once blanketed the state in the past, and many of them existed for centuries before being abandoned or destroyed.

Long before the arrival of the Europeans, some extensive towns existed, such as the one whose remains may still be viewed at Moundville, in Hale County, which was founded about the year 1200 and was abandoned about 1500. The inhabitants of such ancient towns had no written language, so we can only surmise their history from the study of archaeological remains.

Only known historical sites are listed in this volume. Each site is named, and if it had other names, they too are given.

ABIHKA (Abeca, Abika, Abi-Hka). This Upper Creek town was near the Coosa River, south of Tallassehatchee Creek, approximately 2½ miles south of Rendalia, in Talladega County.[1] On De Lisle's map in 1704 the ancient town appeared east of the Coosa River, just north of its influx into Pakan Tallahassee Creek. It was shown on Balen's map in 1733 on the east side of the Coosa but some distance from the river. Because it was in the northern limits of the Creek's country, Abihka may have served as a defense outpost against hostile tribes to the north.[2]

ABIKUDSHI (Abikakutchee). Situated on a mile-wide plain, Abikudshi was approximately a mile from where the Sylacauga

Highway crosses over Tallassehatchee Creek, on the right bank
of the creek, 5 miles east of the Coosa River, in Talladega County.[3] The name of this village means "Little Abihka." Some authorities believe that it was on the same site as the older town; however, the Creeks often moved their villages. It was first listed on
De Crenay's map in 1733. The French census in 1760 showed
the village with a population of 130 warriors.[4] In 1799, Benjamin
Hawkins, the famous Indian agent, reported that the inhabitants
"have no fences, and but few hogs, horses and cattle; they are
attentive to white people, who live among them, and particularly
so to white women."[5]

ANATITCHAPKO (Enitachopko). This Hillabee village was
situated on Anatitchapko Creek, a northern tributary of Hillabee
Creek, 10 miles north of Pinkneyville, in Clay County. The name
of this village means "long swamp," or "long thicket"; probably
it was named for the dense undergrowth in the region.[6]

Only two days after his victory over the Red Sticks in the battle
of Emuckfau, General Andrew Jackson and his Tennessee militia, on January 24, 1814, were ambushed by Red Sticks in a ravine
near this village. While forming a line to protect his men who
had been wounded in the previous battle, Jackson discovered
that his rear guard had panicked and plunged in disorder into
the thicket on the other side of the creek. Only about 100 brave
men remained to fight off the effect of the panic. With renewed
effort the Indians attacked the militiamen who were attempting
to guard the ford of the creek, throwing the force of the charge
against Lieutenant Robert Armstrong's company. The Tennesseans desperately held the position with the aid of a six-pound
cannon.

After regrouping his men, Jackson began to hurl his infantrymen into the ranks of the Red Sticks, and the tide of battle turned
in favor of the whites. The Indians soon retreated into the
forest and were pursued for over 2 miles. Even though they had
been driven from the field of battle, the Red Sticks spread prop-
aganda that they had "whipped Captain Jackson and driven
him to the Coosa River."[7] Jackson buried his dead at this position, then resumed his march to Fort Strother.

APALATCHUKLA (Talua 'Laka). This Lower Creek town was on the west bank of the Chattahoochee River, at Hatcher's Bend, in the eastern section of Russell County.[8] The town was dedicated to peace with the white man. The French census of 1760 listed it with a population of 60 warriors. A year later at a council held at Savannah, the town was reported to have had but 20 hunters. William Bartram, the noted botanist, visited the site in 1777 and described the town as "the ruin of an ancient Indian town and fortress."[9]

ATCHINALGI (Atchina-algi, Genalga). An Upper Creek town, Atchinalgi was probably on the east bank of the Tallapoosa River at or near the mouth of Cedar Creek, in Randolph County. The name of the town means "cedar grove people."[10] In 1796, Benjamin Hawkins stated that the town "is the farthest north of all the Creeks."[11] On November 13, 1813, it was destroyed by General James White and his Tennessee troopers.[12]

ATHAHATCHEE (Athahachi). This site covered a square mile, and was 5/8 mile from the Cahaba River bridge, and 2 miles from the community of Sprott, in Perry County.[13] Rodrigo Ranjel, private secretary of Hernando DeSoto, stated in his diary that the Spaniards had their first audience with the mighty chieftain Tuscaloosa at this village, on October 10, 1540. "The chief was on a kind of balcony on a mound at one side of the square, his head covered by a kind of coif like the almaizal, so that his head-dress was like a Moor's, which gave him an aspect of authority; he also wore a pelote or mantle of feathers down to his feet, very imposing; he was seated on some high cushions, and many of the principal men among his Indians were with him."[14] The following day DeSoto demanded and received 400 carriers for his baggage train, and was promised 100 women when he reached Maubila.[15]

AUTAUGA (Atagi, At-tau-gee, Autobi, Dumplin Town). This village once existed on the west side of the Alabama River, 6 miles below the site of the Indian village of Tawasa, in Autauga County.[16] The Indian agent, Benjamin Hawkins, visited the small village in 1798, and reported that it was "spread out for two miles on the right bank of the river; they have fields on both sides, but their chief dependence is on the left side; . . . the right side of the pine forest extends down to At-tau-gee Creek . . . These people have little intercourse with white people; although they are hospitable . . . They have some hogs, horses and cattle, in a very fine range, perhaps the best on the river . . . "[17] In 1832, Schoolcraft stated that the village had a population of 54 families.[18]

AUTOSSEE (Atasi, Atoches). This Upper Creek town was on the south side of the Tallapoosa River below and adjoining Calibee Creek, some 20 miles above the mouth of the Coosa River, in Macon County.[19] Autossee, meaning "war club," was first mentioned on De Crenay's map in 1733. A problem exists for historians because the Belen map of 1744 showed three locations with this same name. In the French census of 1760 the population of the town was 80 warriors. Bartram visited the site in 1777, and Hawkins in 1798 estimated that the town contained 80 warriors.[20] The inhabitants joined the Red Sticks in 1813 and assisted in the destruction of Fort Mims. The Georgia militia, under the command of General John Floyd, attacked and destroyed Autossee on November 29, 1813.[21]

BLACK WARRIOR'S TOWN (Taska luka, Tuscaloosa). Situated on the banks of the Black Warrior River, this Creek town was possibly at a site which is today just west of the Tuscaloosa Country Club, about 100 yards west of the intersection of Sanders Ferry Road and old Highway 11, in the city of Tuscaloosa.[22] A group of "separatist" Creeks founded the town.

Differing opinions exist pertaining to the site of the town that was burned by General John Coffee. Thomas McAdory Owen stated that the site was at "the Mulberry Fork of the Black Warrior River, opposite the confluence of the Sipsey Fork," in northeast Walker County.[23] More recent investigations, conducted by The University of Alabama, December, 1975–February, 1976, indicated that the site was near Birmingham, in Jefferson County.

In 1811, Tecumseh, the famous Shawnee orator who hoped to bring the Southern Indians to the Red Stick cause, was forced out of the Choctaw Nation because that tribe had no desire to make war on the settlers. A group of Choctaws, under the leadership of David Folsom, a half-breed chief, accompanied the Shawnees to the Tombigbee River, making sure that the hostiles were departing from the Choctaw lands. During the night, while they were camping on the west bank of the river, warriors from Black Warrior's Town attacked the Folsom party without warning, killing several of them.

The chief of Black Warrior's Town, Oce-oche-motla, welcomed Tecumseh to the town, and soon afterwards, the inhabitants voted to join the Red Sticks. In the meantime, David Folsom, after having been wounded at the Tombigbee, returned to his home and formed a war party of Choctaws, who made a raid on Black Warrior's Town, where they stole horses, burned several cabins, and killed a few of the Creeks.

In the spring of 1812, a band of Creeks under Little Warrior returned from a visit with Tecumseh to Detroit. At the mouth of the Duck River in Tennessee these Creeks had killed several whites and had taken a captive, a Mrs. Crawley. The unfortunate woman was sold to Oce-oche-motla, as the war party passed by Black Warrior's Town. Tandy Walker, a government blacksmith and interpreter at St. Stephens, learned that the woman was being held as a prisoner and agreed to attempt to free her. He visited the town on the pretense of hunting for game in the area, and later made a daring escape with the woman by canoe to St. Stephens.[24]

In October, 1813, 800 soldiers under John Coffee destroyed the town. A member of this force, Davy Crockett, described the action: "The Indian town was a large one; but when we arrived we found the Indians had all left it. There was a large field of corn standing out and a pretty good supply in some cribs. There was also a fine quantity of dried beans, which were very acceptable to us; and without delay we secured them as well as the corn, and then burned the town to ashes; after which we left the place."[25]

BODKA VILLAGE. This Choctaw village was situated on both sides of Bodka Creek, 8 miles from Gainesville, in Sumter County. The name means "wide creek." Indians from this village were friends of the traders at Gaines Trading Post, which was near what is today the town of Gainesville. Timmillichee, the chieftain, remained in this vicinity when his tribesmen were forced to move to the West in 1831; he sold the site to John A. Winston, later Governor of Alabama, who was a cotton planter in the county.[26]

CABUSTO (Zabusta). The ancient town, Cabusto, was probably on the west bank of the Black Warrior River at St. Stephens Bluff, in Greene County.[27] Its name means "great water." The DeSoto expedition visited the town on November 24, 1540. Ranjel recorded in his journal that "there we crossed the river in a boat and with some canoes that we found in that place; and we tarried for the night in another village on the other side."[28]

CASISTE. This ancient village was probably on the site of Cahaba, Alabama's first state capital. Much evidence of occupation has been found ½ mile south of the site of the first Capitol building, in Dallas County.[29] On October 5, 1540, Ranjel recorded that the DeSoto party "went on from Talisi and came to Casiste for the night. This was a small village by the river."[30]

CHALAKAGAY (Sylacoggy, Sauwanoos). It was situated near the waterworks of Sylacauga, in Talladega County.[31] The town was established by Shawnee Indians from Ohio in 1748. Ten years later it was reported to contain 80 warriors.[32]

CHANANAGI (Chunnenuggee). In 1909, Peter Brannon, an early authority on Alabama Indian life, located the site of this Lower Creek town "just south of the Central of Georgia Railroad near Suspension," in Bullock County.[33] Very little is known about the town. Chunnenuggee Ridge and Chunnenuggee Camp Ground derive their names from the ancient town.[34]

CHIAHA. On an island in the Tennessee River, this ancient town was near Stevenson, in Jackson County.[35] On June 5, 1540, the DeSoto expedition reached this great town by canoes and rafts. A friendly chieftain offered the Spaniards 20 barns full of corn, bear's oil in gourds, walnut oil, pots of honey, and a string of freshwater pearls, about two yards in length. The Spaniards reported that the temple in the town, where the bones of the Indian's ancestors were deposited, contained a large quantity of valuables.[36]

CHICKASAW TOWN (Chicachas, Tchikachas). This Chickasaw village was on or near the south side of the headwaters of Talladega Creek, just north of Chandler Springs, in Talladega County.[37] It first appeared on the Mitchell map of 1775. The French census taken fifteen years before showed the village with a total population of 200, of which 40 were warriors.[38]

CHISKA TALOFA (Cheskitalo-was). Situated on the western side of the Chattahoochee River, this Lower Creek town was said to be 4 miles below the Indian village of Wikai 'liko, in Henry County.[39] Chiska Talofa was first mentioned in the trade regulations of 1761 as a village of 30 hunters. It was later said to have been a Seminole village containing 580 persons.[40]

CHOLOCCO LITABIXEE (Horseshoe Bend). A famous Upper Creek village, Cholocco Litabixee was in the "Horseshoe Bend" of the Tallapoosa River, 12 miles north of Dadeville, in Tallapoosa County.[41] At this site on March 27, 1814, General Andrew Jackson defeated the hostile Red Sticks under the command of Chief Menawa. The village actually stood on the banks of the river, but the Indians had erected a log breastworks across the peninsula on a ridge to the rear of the village. Jackson made his attack on the breastworks while John Coffee's men swam across the river to the village where they destroyed the Indians' canoes. Almost 1000 warriors were slain in the battle, many of whom were shot as they attempted to swim the river to escape. This battle broke the power of the Red Sticks, and they soon surrendered at Fort Jackson.[42] Today this area is the site of the Horseshoe Bend National Military Park.

COOSA (Cosa, Coca). This ancient town was situated on the east bank of Talladega Creek and its mouth, 1½ miles north-

east of Childersburg, in Talladega County.[43] DeSoto and his
party visited the town from July 16 to August 20, 1540, and reported that it was in a flourishing condition with 500 houses and
over 1000 warriors. "This chief," Ranjel wrote, "is a powerful one
and a ruler of a wide territory."[44]

In June, 1560, some of the followers of the ill-fated expedition
of Don Tristán de Luna visited the town in search of food. They
found a town of only 30 houses in a neighborhood of several
small villages.[45] Juan De Pardo visited the area in 1566 and found
the region to be populous. He described Coosa as a "pueblo",
containing 150 people.[46] William Bartram visited the site in
1775 and stated that the town had been abandoned and was in
ruins.[47]

COSTE. A site now inundated, this ancient town was at the
upper end of Pine Island in the Tennessee River, in Marshall
County.[48] The DeSoto expedition reached this town on July 2,
1540. Ranjel recorded the event of their arrival: "This village
was on an island in the river, which there flows large, swift, and
hard to enter. And the Christians crossed the first branch with no
danger to any of the soldiers, yet it was no small venture careless
and unarmed . . . And when the soldiers began to climb upon
the barbacoas, in an instant the Indians began to take up clubs
and seize their bows and arrows and to go to the open square."[49]

When threatened by the 1,500 warriors, DeSoto immediately
seized the chieftain and about a dozen of the leading men, who
were chained and collared. The threat of burning these captives
caused the warriors to lay down their arms and a battle was
avoided.[50]

CREEK PATH. This Cherokee settlement was situated on the
eastern side of Brown's Creek at the crossing of the present road
from Warrenton to Albertville, about 4 miles southeast of Guntersville, in Marshall County.[51] Established in 1785, Creek Path
soon became a very important community of between 400 and
500 people—one-third of the entire Cherokee population within
the present-day boundaries of Alabama.[52] In 1820 the American
Board of Commissioners of Foreign Missions established a school

and church at Creek Path under the superintendency of the Reverend William Potter. This mission continued in operation until the Cherokees left Alabama for Oklahoma.[53]

CROWTOWN (Kagunyi). Situated on Crow Creek, ½ mile from its confluence with the Tennessee River, this town was approximately 4 miles south of Stevenson, in Jackson County.[54] One of the Five Lower Towns of the Cherokees on the Tennessee River, Crowtown was considered one of the most important towns in the Tennessee Valley. Chickamauga Cherokees under the leadership of "The Crow" founded the town in 1782. These Indians were among the greatest enemies of the white settlers in Tennessee and Kentucky, and probably many raiders set out from the town.[55]

DOUBLEHEAD'S VILLAGE. This village was on the south side of the Tennessee River, near the place where the Natchez Trace crossed the river at Colbert's Ferry, in Colbert County.[56] In 1790 Chief Doublehead founded the village, with the aid of 40 Creek and Cherokee warriors. Doublehead has been called "the most cruel and blood-thirsty of the Indians" who raided the Cumberland settlements of Tennessee. He was killed in 1805 in a tavern brawl.[57]

ECUNCHATI (Ecunchate, Ikan-tchati, Red Ground). On a bluff above the Alabama River, this village was where the city of Montgomery now stands.[58] Its name means "red bluff" or "red ground." This ancient home of the Alabama Indians witnessed the passing of the DeSoto expedition on September 6, 1540.[59]

The French trade regulations of 1761 listed the village with a population of 70 hunters. In 1799, Benjamin Hawkins visited the town and recorded that it was "a small village on the left bank of the Alabama, which has its fields on the right bank in the cane swamp. They are a poor people without stock, are idle and indolent, and seldom make enough bread, but have fine melons in great abundance in their season."[60]

The historian, William Stokes Wyman, wrote that his earliest recollection (1839) of the "town-site itself was a level, uncultivated field, hard by the bluff of the river. The surface was strewn with the remains of the former Indian occupation." Two mounds stood at this site until 1833, one being 25 feet high and 90 feet square.[61]

FAKITCHIPUNTA (Turkey Town). This Choctaw town was situated on both sides of the Tombigbee River (two-thirds of it lying on the eastern bank), in Choctaw and Clarke counties. Turkey Creek flowed into the river about the middle of the northwest quarter of the town.[62]

In 1830 the Treaty of Dancing Rabbit Creek ceded this large town and the surrounding area to the white settlers. At that time it was the last of the Choctaw possessions east of the Tombigbee River.

FUSI-HATCHI (Fuś-Hatchi, Foutchachy). An Upper Creek town on the north bank of the Tallapoosa River, Fusi-Hatchi was 1 mile north of Wares Ferry, in Elmore County.[63] De Crenay, on his map of 1733, placed the town on the south side of the Tallapoosa River, opposite its later position. The French census of 1760 showed that some of the Kusas people had united with this village, giving it a combined population of 60 warriors. The trade regulations of July, 1761, listed the combined population as 50 hunters.[64]

GUNTER'S VILLAGE. This Cherokee village was on the present site of the town of Guntersville, in Marshall County.[65] John Gunter, a Scottish trader, settled among the Cherokees during the American Revolution because of his Tory sentiments, married a Cherokee woman, and was adopted into the tribe. He founded this village in 1784 along a trading path. His double-log home stood "at the foot of the hill" in Guntersville, about 200 yards from the creek. He died in 1835 and is buried in an unknown grave.[66]

HATCHITCHAPA (Hatch-chi-chubba, Hatchechubbee). This Upper Creek village was situated at the headwaters of Mitchell's Creek, a few miles south of Central, in Elmore County.[67] This village was destroyed by Red Sticks in 1813, was evidently rebuilt, and appeared in the census of 1832.[68]

HILLABI. This Upper Creek town was on the left bank of Little Hillabi Creek, somewhat opposite Pinkneyville, near the Clay and Tallapoosa county line.[69] In 1540, DeSoto discovered a tribe of Hillabis living on the lower Savannah River in Georgia. It is quite possible that these Indians later migrated into Alabama. The trade regulations of July, 1761, showed the town with a population of 40 hunters. The town contained peach orchards and also livestock.[70]

During the Creek War of 1813–14, the Hillabis fought against the Tennessee militia at the battles of Tallahasseehatchee and Talladega. After the Indians were defeated in both encounters, a delegation of warriors went to General Jackson at Fort Strother asking for a termination of hostilities. Realizing that an expedition under General James White was at that moment on its way to Hillabi, Jackson attempted to halt the proposed attack, but unfortunately was too late.

On November 18, 1813, General White surrounded the town, which contained 65 wounded warriors who were hospitalized in the cabins there. No battle took place. The militiamen went into each cabin, bayoneting the wounded in their beds. The town was then burned. This needless action seriously hurt Jackson's reputation in the eyes of the friendly Indians, and is referred to in history as the "Hillabi Massacre."[71]

HOITHLEWALLI (Huhliwahli, Ulibahali, Olibahali, Cheeawo ola, Telonalis Chevallis). For several centuries Indians lived at this site on the right bank of the Tallapoosa River, on a strip of land east of the influx of Mitchell's Creek (also known as Chubbehatchee Creek), extending back from the river for a mile, in Elmore County.[72] On August 31, 1540, the DeSoto expedition reached this town, and the Gentleman of Elvas wrote in his diary: "The Governor [DeSoto] ordered all his men to enter the town which was enclosed and near which flowed a small river. The enclosure, like that in other towns seen there afterward, was of thick logs, set solidly close together in the ground, and many long poles as thick as an arm placed crosswise. The height of the enclosure was that of a good lance, and it was plastered within and without and had loopholes."[73]

The town appears on many of the early maps under a variety of names. In the French census of 1760 it appeared with a population of 70 warriors.[74] In 1799, Benjamin Hawkins stated that the more progressive inhabitants of the town had moved to the south side (left bank) of the river, leaving the idlers to the town proper.[75] During the first week in April, 1814, just after the American victory over the Red Sticks at Horseshoe Bend, the Red Sticks abandoned Hoithlewalli and attempted to escape from the encircling armies. The militiamen then destroyed the town along with many others, and it was never occupied again.[76]

HUMATI. This village was probably situated on the west bank of the Alabama River, just north of Camden, in Wilcox County.[77] Thomas McAdory Owen believed the site was on the eastern shore of the Cahaba River, just north of Oakmulgee Creek, in Dallas County.[78] The name means "turkey gobbler," and was possibly the name of the chieftain there in 1540 rather than the name of the village. DeSoto passed through the village on October 7, 1540.[79]

IKANATCHAKA (Holy Ground). An Upper Creek town, Ikanatchaka was on the south side of the Alabama River, between Pintalala and Big Swamp creeks, 2½ miles north of White Hall, and just below the mouth of Holy Ground Creek, in Lowndes County.[80]

William Weatherford, the "Red Eagle," had a large plantation in this vicinity before the Creek War. After becoming an important Red Stick leader (he was in command in the Indian victory at Fort Mims), Weatherford strongly fortified this position and used it as a storehouse for plunder. The prophets there assured the warriors that no white man could come into their town without suffering instant death, and the town soon became a place where white and Indian captives were held, tortured, and burned to death.

On December 23, 1813, General Ferdinand Claiborne and his Mississippi militiamen stormed the position. The Red Sticks fought with considerable fury for a short time, but their line of defense was soon broken, and the survivors fled into the swampland. One white soldier and 30 Red Sticks were killed. Weatherford escaped across the river as Claiborne destroyed the town.[81]

IMUKFA (Emuckfau). On the north or right bank of Imukfa Creek, this Upper Creek town was in the southern section of Clay County.[82] Benjamin Hawkins, who visited the town in 1799, stated that the inhabitants had "fine rich plats on the creek, and a good range for their cattle; they possess some hogs, cattle and horses, and began to be attentive to them."[83]

On the morning of January 22, 1814, the Red Sticks attacked the camp of General Jackson near Imukfa Creek. General John Coffee, with the force of 400 men, saved Jackson's camp by charging into the enemy, driving them for two miles, and then burning their encampment (probably the town of Imukfa). The ferocity of the Indian attack caused Jackson to pull his forces back to Fort Strother on the following day, where fresh supplies and reinforcements could be obtained.[84]

KAILAIDSHI (Kiliga, Killeegko, Kialige, Kiolege). This Upper Creek town was situated near the present-day Prospect Methodist Church, south of Little Kowaligi Creek, a mile west of the community of Kowaligi, in Elmore County.[85] The name of the town means "the warrior's headdress." Tecumseh, the Shawnee chieftain, visited the town in 1811 and addressed the inhabitants while standing on a seven-foot-high stone. When the villagers decided to remain friendly with the whites, Red Sticks burned the town. Probably it was later rebuilt; it appeared in the census taken in the 1830s.[86]

KAWITA TALAHASSI (Old Coweta, Lower Kawita, Caouritas). This Lower Creek town was situated a half mile west of the Chattahoochee River on the south side of Broken Arrow Creek, in Russell County. Fort Mitchell is only 2 miles northeast of this site.[87] On the De Lisle map of 1707, the Kawitas were situated in a broad area from the west bank of the Chattahoochee to the Flint River in Georgia. The Chattahoochee was listed as the "Riviere des Caouitas" on the De Crenay map of 1733. Probably the Kawitas did live east of the Chattahoochee for many years with their lands extending over a broad region.[88] The French census of 1760 showed the town (in its Alabama location) with a population of 150 warriors. The British trade regulations of 1761 listed the town with 150 hunters.[89]

In 1775, William Bartram visited the town and recorded: "The great Coweta town . . . is called the bloody town, where the Micos chiefs and warriors assemble when a general war is proposed, and here captives and state malefactors are put to death."[90]

Benjamin Hawkins, in 1799, wrote that "the town is half a mile from the river, on the right bank of the creek; it is on a high flat, bordered on the east by the flats of the river, and west by broken hills; they have but a few settlers in the town; the fields are on a point of land three-quarters of a mile below the town . . . They estimate their number of gun men at one hundred; but the agent has ascertained, by actual enumeration, that they have but sixty-six . . . "[91]

During the Creek War of 1813–14, the inhabitants of this town not only remained at peace with the whites, but also fought against the Red Sticks. Their chieftain, William McIntosh, and his warriors joined General John Floyd's Georgia militiamen and fought bravely at the battles of Autossee and Horseshoe Bend. After the war, McIntosh was instrumental in getting treaties signed ceding Creek lands to the United States Government, therefore many Creeks believed that he had betrayed them and killed him on April 30, 1825.[92]

KAXA. This ancient village was on the Alabama River just south of the mouth of Cedar Creek, in Dallas County.[93] Very little is known about Kaxa. DeSoto stopped there on October 6, 1540, and Ranjel described it as "a wretched village on the river banks on the direct line from Talisi to Tascaluca."[94]

KOASATI (Coosauda, Coshattee, Coassati, Coosau-dee). This famous town was situated on the west bank of the Alabama River a few miles below the junction of the Coosa and Tallapoosa rivers (Hawkins stated that it was 3 miles below the junction), in Elmore

County.[95] The town was once the home of the Alabamas (Alibamons), the southernmost group of Upper Creeks, who had a number of villages in the area. In the early years of the French colony at Mobile, the Alabamas were quite hostile to the French. Their attitude changed during the Yamasee War of 1715–16 with the British, and the chieftain of this town asked the French to build a fort at the junction of the Coosa and Tallapoosa (see Fort Toulouse in Part II).[96]

During the 1790s, the chieftain of this town, Captain Isaacs, made raids against the Cumberland settlements in Tennessee, but he later became a strong friend of the Americans. After refusing to join the Red Stick movement in 1811, he was killed along with several other members of his tribe in the summer of 1813. The following year the town was destroyed by Lieutenant-Colonel John H. Gibson after it had become a refuge for Red Sticks.[97]

KULUMI (Coulommie, Colomin, Culloomi, Coolome). Situated on high ground ½ mile from the Tallapoosa River, this Upper Creek town was just west of old Ware's Ferry, in Elmore County.[98] The town first appeared on the De Crenay map of 1733. Other maps showed it on the Altamaha or on the Chattahoochee rivers, perhaps proving that the town had earlier been in different locations.

The French census of 1760 listed the town with a population of 50 warriors. In 1791, William Bartram stated that the town had originally stood on the east side of the Tallapoosa River, but that the more recent town was on a ridge on the opposite shore. He also observed that "their houses are neat, commodious buildings, a wooden frame with plastered walls, and roofed with cypress bark or shingles; every habitation consists of four oblong square houses, of one story . . . situated as to form an exact square, encompassing an area of court yard of about a quarter of an acre of ground, leaving an entrance into it at each corner . . . "[99]

LALOKALKA (Thlot-lo-gul-gau). This village was on a pond-like creek, believed to be Jack's Creek, an upper branch of Elkehatchee, about 14 miles from its junction with the Tallapoosa River, in Coosa County.[100] The name of this village means "fish separated." Thomas McAdory Owen stated that this village was the home of Hannah Hale, a white woman who had been captured by the Indians when she was a child. She later married the headman of this village, and by him had five children. In 1799, at the national council of the Creek Nation, an agent was appointed to watch out for the welfare of this woman and her children.[101]

LITTAFUCHEE. An Upper Creek town, Littafuchee was situated on the south bank of Big Canoe Creek, 8 miles north of Ashville, in St. Clair County.[102] The name means "making of arrows." Very little is known about the history of the town. On October 29, 1813, Colonel Dyer and his Tennesseans surrounded and captured this position, taking 29 prisoners and destroying the town.[103]

MAUBILA (Mabila, Mavila). The site of one of the most exciting encounters in Alabama history, the Battle of Maubila, is unknown. Although historians and archaeologists have searched for it for well over a century, Maubila continues to elude them and remains as mysterious as ever.

Three members of the DeSoto expedition, Rodrigo Ranjel, the leader's private secretary, Luys Hernandez de Biedma, the commissory, and the "Gentleman of Elvas," a soldier, all kept diaries or wrote narratives pertaining to the great town and battle fought there,[104] which have been studied by historians. Albert James Pickett, the antebellum historian, was "satisfied that Maubila was upon the north bank of the Alabama, and at a place now called Choctaw Bluff, in the county of Clarke, about twenty-five miles above the confluence of the Alabama and Tombigby."[105] H. S. Halbert, famous for his history of Clarke County and of the Creek Indian War, placed the site near Forkland in southern Greene County, which seems unnecessarily far to the north.[106] Peter Hamilton, author of *Colonial Mobile*, partially agreed with Pickett, locating Maubila somewhere near the northern boundary of Clarke County.[107] A. B. Moore, in his *History of Alabama*, stated that research had determined the site to be in either Wilcox or Marengo counties.[108] The final report of the United States DeSoto Commission, submitted to Congress in 1939, conceded that the elusive site was probably somewhere in southern Marengo County.[109]

In 1973, Dalton Smith, a supervisor for the Adams Lumber Company, discovered a large site some 8 miles north of Choctaw Bluff, northwest of Gainestown, 5 miles from the Alabama River, in south central Clarke County.[110] Immediately many history buffs were encouraged to believe that Maubila had finally been found. But after making an investigation, Dr. Walter B. Jones, former state geologist, stated that he did not believe the site was Maubila, but it was his opinion that the site of Maubila was "on the north side of Hal's Lake, and, he added, "was probably covered by four or five feet of silt because the area is subject to flooding."[111]

Over ninety years ago, the vicinity of Gainestown was investigated by Dr. Edward Palmer, of the Bureau of American Ethnology, as the possible site of Maubila. He wrote that Maubila was situated at French's or Brashear's Landing, some 4½ miles east of Gainestown, on the north bank of the Alabama River, but added that "all traces of Fort Maubila have disappeared, and the mound once here has disappeared—while the so called burying ground has nearly disappeared, it being on the bank of the river which now caves in, so that but 20 feet of the part of the river bank with human remains is left."[112] Unfortunately, recent investigations have been unable to find Palmer's site, probably because of flooding in 1886, which changed the course of the river.[113]

In 1540, the town of Maubila stood on a plain above the river. Pickett has written that it contained "eighty handsome houses, each capacious enough to contain a thousand men. They were encompassed by a high wall, made of immense trunks of trees, set deep in the ground and close together, strengthened with cross-timbers, and interwoven with large vines. A thick mud plaster, resembling handsome masonry, concealed the wood work, while port-holes were abundant, together with towers, capable of containing eight men each, at a distance of fifty paces apart. An eastern and a western gate opened into the town."[114]

The great chieftain of the region was Tuscaloosa (Tascaluca), who was described as "very tall of body, large limbed, lean, and well built."[115] In May, 1539, Hernando DeSoto, commanding 1,000 men, landed at Tampa Bay and proceeded northward through Florida, Georgia, and the Carolinas, then marched southwestward across Tennessee, and into Alabama, in search of riches for the glory of Spain. After a year of hardships, he marched southward to the Alabama River, then followed the river into the southwestern part of Alabama. On October 10 he had his first meeting with Chief Tuscaloosa at Athahatchee (see Athahatchee).

On October 18, 1540, DeSoto had his second and last confrontation with Tuscaloosa, this time in the town of Maubila. Luys Hernandez de Biedma described what happened on that fatal day:

"At nine o'clock, one morning, we arrived at Mavila, a small town very strongly stockaded, situated on a plain. We found the Indians had demolished some habitations about it, to present a clear field. A number of the chiefs came out to receive us as soon as we were in sight, and they asked the Governor [DeSoto], through an interpreter, if he would like to stop on that plain, or preferred to enter the town, and said that in the evening they would give us the Indians to carry burdens. It appeared to our Chief better to go thither with them, and he commanded that all should enter the town, which we did.

"Having come within the enclosure, we walked about, talking with the Indians, supposing them to be friendly, there were not over three or four hundred in sight, though full five thousand were in the town, whom we did not see, nor did they show themselves at all. Apparently rejoicing, they began their customary songs and dances; and some 15 or 20 women having performed before us a little while, for dissimulation, the Cacique [Tuscaloosa] got up and withdrew into one of the houses. The Governor sent to tell him that he must come out, to which he answered that he would not; and the Captain of the body-guard entered the door to bring him forth, but seeing many Indians present, fully prepared for battle, he thought it best to withdraw and leave him. He reported that the houses were full of men, ready with bows and arrows, bent on some mischief. The Governor called to an

Indian passing by, who also refused to come, a gentleman near took him by the arm to bring him, when, receiving a push, such as to make him let go his hold, he drew his sword and dealt a stroke in return that cleaved away an arm.

"With the blow they all began to shoot arrows at us, some from within the houses, through the many loop-holes they had arranged, and some from without. As we were so wholly unprepared, having considered ourselves on a footing of peace, we were obliged from the great injuries we were sustaining, to flee from the town, leaving behind all that the carriers had brought for us, as they had there set down their burdens. When the Indians saw that we had gone out, they closed the gates, and beating their drums, they raised flags, with great shouting; then, emptying our knapsacks and bundles, showed up above the palisades all we had brought, as much as to say that they had those things in possession. Directly as we retired, we bestrode our horses and completely encircled the town, that none might thence anywhere escape. The Governor directed that 60 of us should dismount, and that 80 of the best accoutred should form in 4 parties, to assail the place on as many sides, and the first of us getting in should set fire to the houses, that no more harm should come to us: so we handed over our horses to other soldiers who were not in armour, that if any Indians should come running out of the town they might overtake them.

"We entered the town and set it on fire, whereby a number of Indians were burned, and all that we had was consumed, so that there remained not a thing. We fought that day until night-fall, without a single Indian having surrendered to us—they fighting bravely like lions. We killed them all, either with fire or the sword, or, such of them as came out, with the lance, so that when it was nearly dark there remained only three alive; and these, taking the women that had been brought to dance, placed the 20 in front, who, crossing their hands, made signs to us that we should come for them. The Christians advanced toward the women, these turned aside, and the 3 men behind them shot their arrows at us, when we killed 2 of them. The last Indian, not to surrender, climbed a tree that was in the fence, and taking a cord from his bow, tied it about his neck, and from a limb hanged himself."[116]

Biedma stated that 20 Spainards were killed and 250 were wounded. Ranjel numbered the Spanish casualties at 22 killed and 148 wounded, while he estimated the Indian losses at 3,000. The Gentleman of Elvas stated that 18 of DeSoto's men were killed and 150 wounded, while the total number of dead on the field of battle was 2,500.[117] DeSoto and his men remained on the battle site attending to their wounded until November 14, when they marched northwestward toward Mississippi.

MUKLASA (Amooklasah). This Upper Creek town was on the left bank of Eight Mile Branch, 1½ miles from the south bank of the Tallapoosa River, in Montgomery County.[118] The French census of 1760 listed this town as being 3 leagues from Fort Toulouse and with a population of 50 men. The following year the English trade regulations showed the town's population with 30 hunters.[119]

The most famous chieftain of Muklasa was Wolf King, who served as the spokesman for both the Upper and Lower Creeks at a council with Sir Henry Ellis, Governor of Georgia, at Savannah in November, 1757. On April 30, 1761, the town was the meeting place for chiefs from twelve Upper Creek towns, where joint action was agreed upon to stand with the English against the French.[120]

In 1791, Benjamin Hawkins described Muklasa as being located "on the left bank of a fine little creek, and bordering on a cypress swamp; their fields are below those of Sauvannogee, bordering on the river; they have some lots about their houses fenced for potatoes; one chief has some cattle, horses and hogs; a few others have some cattle and hogs . . ."[121]

NANIPACNA (Nanih pakna). Many historians believe that this town was situated on Boykin's Ridge, on Pine Barren Creek, on the east side of the Alabama River, in the northern section of Wilcox County.[122] The name of the town means "hill top" in the Choctaw language. In 1560, the ill-fated expedition of Don Tristán de Luna reached this town, found it deserted, but discovered there a large supply of corn, beans, and other needed provisions. The inhabitants, who had fled into the forest minutes before the arrival of the Spaniards, soon returned and made the visitors welcome. Much to the Indians' regret, the uninvited guests showed no inclination to leave, and the food supply soon vanished, forcing all the people to search for wild food during the winter in order to survive. The town last appeared on De Crenay's map in 1733.[123]

NAUCHE (Natchez, Nau-chee, Naotche). This town was on Tallasseehatchee Creek, 4 miles west of Sycamore, in Talladega County. It was situated on a rich flat of land just below a fork in the creek.[124] The Natchez Indians originally were on the lower Mississippi River. Warfare with the French had so reduced their ranks that they were forced to abandon their villages in 1729 and take refuge with other tribes. The largest body of these refugees founded the town of Nauche on Tallasseehatchee Creek.[125]

In 1799, Benjamin Hawkins stated that the "settlements are scattered on both sides of the creek for two miles; they have no worm fences, and but little stock. One chief, a brother of Chin-a-be, has a large stock of hogs, and had ninety fit for market, in 1798 . . . They estimate their number of gunmen at one hundred; but they are, probably, not more than fifty . . . "[126] During the Creek War of 1813–14, the inhabitants of Nauche remained peaceful and refused to join the Red Stick movement. They migrated to the West in 1832.[127]

NIUYAKA. An Upper Creek town, Niuyaka was situated on the south bank of the Tallapoosa River near the point where Eagle Creek flows into the river, in Tallapoosa County.[128] Hawkins stated that "these people lived formerly at Tote-paufcau, on Chat-to-ho-che, and moved thence in 1777. They would not take part in the war between the United States and Great Britain [the American Revolution], and determined to retire from their settlements, which, through the rage of war, might feel the effects of the resentment of the people of the United States, when roused by the conduct of the red people, as they were placed between the combatants. The town is on a flat, bordering on the river . . . Some of the people have settled out from the town, and they have good land on Inn-nook-fau creek, which joins the right side of the river, two miles below the town."[129]

ODSHIAPOFA (Hickory Ground, O-che-au-po-fau). This Upper Creek town was on the east bank of the Coosa River approximately 2 miles north of the point where the Coosa and Tallapoosa join to form the Alabama River, in Elmore County.[130] Here the Scotch trader, Lachlan McGillivray, married the beautiful half-breed, Sehoy Marchand, in 1745. Soon afterwards he established a trading post at Little Talisi, 4 miles to the north on the Coosa, where their famous son, Alexander McGillivray, was born.[131]

In 1799, Benjamin Hawkins stated that there were 40 warriors residing at Odshiapofa, and that "three and a half miles above the town are ten apple trees planted by the late General McGillivray [Alexander McGillivray died in Pensacola, February 17, 1793]; half a mile further up are the remains of Old Tal-e-see, formerly the residence of Lochlan [sic] McGillivray and his son, the general. Here are ten apple trees planted by the father, and a stone chimney, the remains of a house built by the son, and these are all the improvements left by the father and son."[132]

In 1802, the national council of the Creek Nation was transferred to Odshiapofa from Tukabatchi. An American town called Jackson was established on this site in 1816, but it was abandoned a few years later.[133]

OKA KAPASSA. Situated just west of Tuscumbia, this Cherokee village was on the west bank of Coldwater (Spring) Creek, at its confluence with the Tennessee River, in Colbert County.[134] The name means "Coldwater Town." The village was established around 1780 as a trading post with the French from the Wabash country, and also as a base from which war parties would set out for the Cumberland settlements in Tennessee.[135]

The Tennesseans went on the offensive in June, 1787, when 130 men assembled at Nashville, under the command of Colonel James Robertson, and promptly set out for the Muscle Shoals area. Five miles from the village of Oka Kapassa the whites came upon the Indians' cornfields along Coldwater Creek. Most of the invaders crossed the creek and entered the edge of the village among a number of log cabins some 300 yards from the river. Seeing them, the Indians ran for their canoes or plunged into the creek. Robertson's men fired a deadly volley into the retreating Indians, killing many of them in the water. The head French trader and 6 of his men were captured along with many valuable supplies. The village was then burned and the livestock was butchered.[136]

OKCHAYI (Okchanya, Oakchoys Old Town, Hookchoie, Oxiaille). This Upper Creek town was situated 6 or 7 miles east of Nixburg, in Coosa County. It stood on the banks of Okchayi Creek, which is today a branch of Kailaidshi Creek, some 5 miles above its junction with the Tallapoosa River.[137] Captain Raymond Demere, an officer of the British Army, mentioned the town in a letter written on November 25, 1756, when he described a council held by the French and the Indians at Fort Toulouse. The French census of 1760 listed the town with a population of 130 warriors, while a year later the British trade regulations showed it with 90 hunters. Governor White of Georgia met there in 1763 to discuss the boundary problem.[138]

OKCHAYUDSHI (Ouchanya, Little Okchayi). On the east bank of the Coosa River, this Upper Creek Village was ¼ mile from Fort Toulouse, in Elmore County. It was said to have been between Hickory Ground and Taskigi.[139] The town was of Alabama (Alibamu) origin. On the Danville map of 1732 it was shown to be on the opposite side of the Coosa from its later location. The French census of 1760 listed it as having 100 warriors, while the British trade regulations of 1761 showed it with two divisions: 20 hunters at Little Oakchoys and 35 hunters opposite Fort Toulouse.[140]

When the French were forced to abandon Fort Toulouse in 1763, the Indians mentioned in the above two divisions were granted permission by the British to migrate and build a settlement on the west side of the Tombigbee River, but they returned to their ancient town sites in 1767. During the Indian war with the Chickasaws in 1793, Okchayudshi was moved across the river and settled between the towns of Hickory Ground and Talisi.[141]

Hawkins visited the village in 1799, and wrote that the inhabitants had "a good stock of hogs, and a few cattle and horses . . . they have fenced all the small fields about their houses, where they raise their peas and potatoes . . . "[142]

OKONI. Approximately 2 miles southeast of the community of Lofton, this Lower Creek town was on the west bank of the Chattahoochee River, near the influx of Snake Creek, in Russell County.[143] It is believed that the inhabitants of this town were Apalachians of the Hitchiti-Mikasuki dialect, who had abandoned their original homeland around 1710. After several removals, they established themselves on the Chattahoochee. The French census of 1760 listed the "Okonis" with a population of 50 warriors.[144]

OPIL AKO (Pitlako). This Upper Creek town was in the Pintablocco Creek swamp, 20 miles upstream from the Coosa River, near Nixburg, in Coosa County.[145] Very little is known about the town. The name means "big swamp." The French census of 1760 listed it with a population of 40 warriors.[146]

OSOTCHI (Hooseche, Ositchy). A Lower Creek town, Osotchi was situated on the south bank of Uchee Creek, approximately 1½ miles above the influx with the Chattahoochee River, in Russell County.[147] The inhabitants of this town originally lived on the banks of the Flint River in Georgia. The town was later moved to Uchee Creek adjacent to the Indian town of Chiaha.[148] Colonel Marinus Willett addressed the Lower Creek leaders at Osotchi on May 17, 1790, extending an invitation from President George Washington for the chiefs to come to a council to be held in New York, where the "Great White Father" would make a treaty with the Indians "as strong as the hills and as lasting as the rivers."[149]

PAKANA (Pacana, Packana, Pakkana, Puckanaw). This Alabama (Alibamu) town was on the north side of the Tallapoosa

River near the site of Fort Toulouse, in Elmore County.[150] Various ancient maps show the town in different locations. The inhabitants of the town were among those who invited the French to build a trading post in the Alabama Country. This post, "Fort Toulouse des Alibamons," was erected in 1717. The French census of 1760 stated that the town was only 300 paces from the fort and had a population of 50 warriors. The English trade regulations of the following year listed "Puckanaw joining Alabama Fort" with 30 hunters.[151]

PAKAN TALAHASSI (Pacana talache, Puckantala). Originally situated near the Coosa River, on the south bank of Walnut Creek, opposite Pakana Talahassi Creek, in Coosa County, this village was later moved across the Coosa River to Pakana Talahassi Creek, 1½ miles southwest of Thorsby, in Chilton County.[152] On the De Crenay map of 1733, this town appeared on both sides of the Coosa River near the confluence of Hatchett Creek. The French census of 1760 listed the town as being 15 leagues from Fort Toulouse, and with a population of 50 warriors.[153]

PIACHI. The ancient village of Piachi was probably situated on the eastern bank of the Alabama River, on a high bluff where the town of Claiborne later stood, in Monroe County.[154] However, fifty years ago historians believed the site was on a high bluff on the eastern bank of the Black Warrior River (the same site as the dead town of Erie), near the community of Sawyerville, in Hale County.[155] The DeSoto expedition reached Piachi on October 13, 1540. Ranjel stated that it "is a village high above a gorge of a mountain stream; and the chief of this place was evil intentioned, and attempted to resist their passage; and as a result, they crossed the stream with effort, and two Christians were slain, and also the principal Indians who accompanied the chief . . ."[156]

QUILBY (Koi albi, Quilby Town). This Choctaw town was on both sides of Quilby Creek, 400 yards above its mouth, in Sumter County.[157] Little historical information exists in regard to this town. The name means "panther killed there." It was abandoned in 1831 when the Choctaws moved to the West.[158]

SAUTA (Santa). This small Cherokee village was near the mouth of North Santa Creek, approximately 5 miles from Scottsboro, in Jackson County.[159] Sauta was founded about 1784. Tradition states that Sequoyah first made known his new invention, the Cherokee alphabet, at Sauta. Later the Episcopal Mission School was established there.[160]

SAWANOGI (Petit Chaouanons, Sawanoki, Souvanoga). A Shawnee town situated on the south side of the Tallapoosa River, 2 miles above Likasa Creek, Sawanogi was near Ware's Ferry, in Montgomery County.[161] It was part of the Creek confederacy. The French census of 1760 listed the town as "Little Shawnees," a town located 3 leagues from Fort Toulouse, with a population of 50 warriors. The British trade regulations of 1761 stated that it contained only 30 hunters.[162]

In 1799, Benjamin Hawkins wrote that the inhabitants were industrious, worked in cornfields, and raised horses and hogs. The fields, he stated, were on both sides of the river.[163] During the Creek War of 1813–14, Sawanogi was a Red Stick town. The antebellum historian, Pickett, said that it was the home of Savannah Jack, "the most blood-thirsty, fiendish and cruel white man that ever inhabited any country."[164]

SAWOKLI (Chaouakale, Chauakle, Sauwoogelo, Great Sawokli, Saukli, Chewakala). This Lower Creek town was on the west bank of the Chattahoochee River, just up from the mouth of Hatchichubbee Creek, in Russell County.[165] Sawokli first appeared on De Crenay's map in 1733. The French census of 1760 listed the town as being 31 leagues from Fort Toulouse and containing a population of 50 men. In 1832, the town was under the control of 2 chieftains and consisted of 56 families. The name appears in a variety of forms on old maps, but its meaning is "raccoon town."[166]

SUKA-ISPOKA (Suk-at-Ispoka). This Upper Creek village was situated on the right bank of the Tallapoosa River, between Welch and Whaley ferries, 12 miles upstream from Okfuski, in Tallapoosa County.[167] The name of this village means "hog gathering place." Probably a branch of the Indian town of Ok-fuski, this village appeared on Mitchell's map in 1755. In the French census of 1760, it was listed along with Okfuski, the combined two having 300 warriors. The British trade regulations of the following year showed it alone with 130 hunters. A white trader was killed in this village on May 14, 1760.[168] Benjamin Hawkins, in 1799, found but few inhabitants living in the village. He stated that the others had moved away to Imukfa.[169]

TALATIGI (Kalalekis). The site of this Upper Creek town was within the present-day limits of Talladega, in Talladega County.[170] The word "Talatigi" means "border town." The French census of 1760 listed this town with a population of 30 warriors.[171]

In November, 1813, many friendly Creeks took refuge in Fort Lashley, which was erected at Talatigi. They were surrounded by 1,000 hostile Red Sticks, who demanded that they surrender. During the night, Selocta Chinnabee, a well-known scout, slipped out of the fort, dressed in a hog skin, crawled through the enemy line, and reached General Andrew Jackson at Fort Strother, telling of their plight.[172] On November 9, Jackson's army, consisting of 1,200 infantrymen and 800 cavalrymen, surrounded the enemy. A battle ensued in which 15 militiamen were killed. The bodies of 299 of the Red Sticks were later counted.[173]

TALI. This ancient village was on McKee's Island, in the Tennessee River, near Guntersville, in Marshall County. The site has been inundated by the river.[174] On July 9, 1540, the chieftain of this village tried in vain to send the women and children across the river in canoes to safety after learning that Spanish soldiers under DeSoto were approaching. However, as Ranjel recorded on the occasion, "the Governor [DeSoto] forced them all to turn back." The chief was then forced to furnish DeSoto's party with canoes in order to enter the village.[175]

TALIMACHUSY. Situated at the mouth of Emauhee Creek, at the point where it enters Tallaseehatchee Creek, this ancient town was just to the east of the highway linking Talladega and

Sylacauga, 4 miles north of the latter city, in Talladega County.[176] Rodrigo Ranjel, the private secretary of Hernando DeSoto, wrote: "On Friday, August 20 [1540], the Governor [DeSoto] and his people left Coca, and there stayed behind a Christian named Feryada, a Levantine. They slept the next night beyond Talimachusy."[177]

TALISHATCHIE. This town was on the eastern side of a small tributary of Tallasseehatchee Creek, 3 miles southwest of Jacksonville, in Calhoun County.[178] In 1813, this Upper Creek town contained 100 families. The Tennessee militia, under John Coffee, dispersed a group of Red Sticks at Talishatchie on November 3, 1813.[179]

TALISI, OLD (Telechys). An Upper Creek town, Talisi was situated on the east bank of the Tallapoosa River, just above the confluence of Yufabi Creek, near the Tallapoosa and Macon county line.[180] Two of the early maps of Alabama, De Crenay's map of 1733 and Belen's map of 1744, placed the town on the west side of the Tallapoosa. On Mitchell's map of the British colonies (1755) it appeared on the eastern side of the river.[181]

In 1799, Benjamin Hawkins found the old town almost deserted, the inhabitants having moved to homes along Yufabi Creek, where they were raising hogs, cattle, and horses.[182] Tecumseh visited the area in 1811 and won many converts to the Red Stick cause. These warriors were among the Red Stick forces at the battles of Autossee and Calebee.[183]

TALISI. This ancient town was on the Alabama River at Durant's Bend, near the Tyler-Benton crossroads, 15 miles northeast of Selma, in Dallas County.[184] DeSoto reached this town on September 17, 1540. His private secretary wrote that "this village is extensive and abounding in corn and near a large river."[185] At Talisi DeSoto received the son of the great chief Tuscaloosa. On September 25, the chief of Talisi gave the Spaniards men and women to carry their baggage, and in return DeSoto released the chieftain of Coosa. The Spanish invaders departed from this town on October 5.[186]

TAMALI (Tum-mult-lau). This Lower Creek town was situated on the Chattahoochee River 7 miles above Ocheesee Bluff, in Barbour County.[187] Tamali appeared on De Crenay's map in 1733. Benjamin Hawkins, in 1799, stated that the town was in an area of swamps containing alligators.[188]

TASKIGI (Les Taskegui, Takiki, Tasquiki, Tastekis, Tuskegee). Established on the banks of the Coosa, this Upper Creek town was just below the site of Fort Toulouse, near the confluence of the Coosa and the Tallapoosa rivers, in Elmore County.[189] Its name means "the seat of the wind." The town was on De Lisle's map of 1707 on the left bank of the Coosa, as it later was found on the maps of De Crenay (1733) and Danville (1732). The French census of 1760 showed the town with a population of 50 warriors, while the English trade regulations of 1761 showed it with 40 hunters.[190]

In 1799, Benjamin Hawkins said that there were "thirty buildings in the town, compactly situated, and from the bluff a fine view of the flat lands in the fork . . . which river is here two hundred yards wide. In the yard of the town house, there are five cannon of iron, with the trunions broke off, and on the bluff are some brickbats, the only remains of the French establishment here . . . The fields are on the left side of Tal-la-poo-sa, and there are some small patches well formed in the fork of the rivers, on the flat rich land below the bluff."[191]

In 1803, the Spanish authorities from Pensacola along with the United States Government, represented by Benjamin Hawkins, plotted to capture the notorious freebooter, William Augustus Bowles. Bowles and a number of Creek chieftains were invited to a great feast at Taskigi. During the festivities Bowles was seized, sent to Mobile by canoe, from whence he was conveyed to Moro Castle in Havana, where he died as a prisoner.[192]

TASQUI. This ancient town was situated in Section 14, Township 17 South, Range 4 East, on the left bank of Choccolocco Creek, about 9 miles from its junction with the Coosa River, in Talladega County.[193] The DeSoto expedition reached Tasqui on July 14, 1540, and spent the night there. Ranjel called the creek a "river," for the creek is 200 feet wide at this crossing point.[194]

TAWASA (Tuasi, Teouachis, Touachys, Touacha, Tawwassa). This Alibamu town was on the northern bluff overlooking the Alabama River, approximately 5 miles north of the bridge on the Birmingham highway, on the Maxwell Field golf course, in Montgomery County.[195] On September 6, 1540, Rodrigo Ranjel, of the DeSoto party, recorded in his diary: "Monday, we came to Tuasi, where we were given carriers and 32 Indian women." After a visit of a week in the town, the Spaniards moved westward.[196]

Many years later, inhabitants of this town moved far to the south, at the confluence of the Alabama and Tombigbee rivers, where they were friends of the French colonists of Mobile. The De Crenay map of 1733 showed them living on the east bank of the Coosa, approximately 12 miles above Witumka. The French census of 1760 listed the town as lying 7 leagues from Fort Toulouse, and containing a population of only 10 warriors.[197]

THLOBLOCCO (Thlobiocco). This Upper Creek village was situated on Thloblocco Creek, a tributary of Cubahatchee Creek, 4 miles east of the highway between Montgomery and Tuskegee (U.S. 80), in Macon County.[198] Very little is known about the village, except that Tustenaggee Emathla ("Jim Boy") made his home there from the mid 1830s until his death in 1851. A Red Stick leader of the Autossees during the Creek War of 1813–14, he served the Americans with distinction against the Seminoles in Florida.[199]

TOMONPA (Tomopa). An ancient Alibamu town, Tomonpa was on the west bank of the Coosa River, opposite Fort Toulouse, in Elmore County.[200] Very little is known about the history of the town. It appeared on Danville's map in 1732 and on De Crenay's map in 1733. The French census of 1760 listed it with a population of 70 warriors. It was later overshadowed by its powerful neighboring town, Witumka.[201]

TUKABATCHI (Totepache, Tuckabatchee, Tugibaxtchi, Tukipahtchi, Tukipaxtchi). This Upper Creek town was on the west bank of the Tallapoosa River, approximately 2½ miles below the falls, just below Tallassee, in Elmore County.[202] The early maps indicate that this town was moved a number of times. The French census of 1760 stated that it lay 10 leagues from Fort Toulouse and contained a population of 200 warriors. The following year it was listed in the English trade regulations in combination with Pea Creek and several plantations with only a population of 90 hunters.[203] Hawkins, in 1799, said that it contained 116 warriors.[204]

Around the year 1812, Big Warrior, the chief of this town, became the Speaker of the Upper Creeks, and Tukabatchi became the capital of the Creek Nation.[205] Tecumseh addressed 5,000 people there in 1811, exhorting them to make war on the whites. However, Big Warrior was a steadfast friend of the Americans, so the Shawnee failed to stimulate the Indians into making war on the settlers.[206]

Civil war came to the lands of the Upper Creeks when 29 towns joined the Red Stick movement and only 5 remained friendly with the Americans. Big Warrior sought means of reuniting the tribe, but a council of Red Sticks condemned the chieftain and 6 of his followers to die. A fort was erected at Tukabatchi, which was later besieged until saved by friendly Creeks from Coweta.[207] After the war, the town became the largest of the Upper Creek towns. The census of 1832 showed it to contain 386 houses.[208]

TURKEY TOWN. Situated in a bend of the Coosa River, this Cherokee town was opposite and 1 mile south of Centre, in Cherokee County.[209] The town was established around 1770. Many raids were organized there under "The Turkey" to strike the settlements in Tennessee and Kentucky.[210] In November, 1813, a detachment of Tennessee militiamen, belonging to the command of General John Cocke, used the town as a base from which they set out to fight the Red Sticks, with the Cherokees enlisted on the American side.[211]

UXAPITA. This ancient town was situated at the mouth of Pursley Creek, at its junction with the Alabama River, 8 miles southwest of Camden, in Wilcox County.[212] The DeSoto expedition visited Uxapita on October 8, 1540, and described it as a "new town."[213]

WAKO KAYI (Acocayes, Waccoy, Ouako kayes). Although this town was moved several times, the most important site of this Upper Creek town was on Flat Top Mountain, on the west fork of Hatchett Creek, in the vicinity of Chambers Spring, in northwestern Clay County.[214] In 1733, De Crenay's map showed the town on Chestnut Creek in Chilton County. Eleven years later Belen placed it on Potchushatche Creek between the Coosa and Tallapoosa rivers. The French census of 1760 stated that it was 15 leagues from Fort Toulouse, and contained a population of 100 warriors, while the British trade regulations of 1761 said that the town consisted of 60 hunters.[215] In 1799, Benjamin Hawkins wrote that the inhabitants "have some horses, hogs and cattle . . ."[216]

WEEMOOKA (Wi-wux-ka, Wewoka, Weowoka, Wewocau, Ouyouka). The site of this Upper Creek town was on the left bank of Wewoka Creek, 4 miles from the Coosa River, in Elmore County.[217] The name means "roaring waters." Little is known about the history of the town. The British trade regulations of 1761 stated that 40 hunters resided there.[218]

WEOGUFKI. This Upper Creek village was situated on Weogufki Creek, about 5 miles above its confluence with Hatchett Creek, in Coosa County.[219] Very little is known about the village other than the fact that it was founded by Indians from the town of Wako Kayi. The census of 1832 listed 132 heads of families residing there.[220]

WILL'S TOWN. This Cherokee town was on Big Will's Creek, just above the community of Lebanon, 6 miles south of Fort Payne, in De Kalb County.[221] Established around 1770, the town was named in honor of the chief, Red-Headed Will. During the

American Revolution, Colonel Alexander Campbell, the British agent to the Cherokees, resided at Will's Town.[222]

WITUMKA (Wetumpka Council House). The site of this Lower Creek town has often been disputed because of frequent changes found on the early maps of the area. A survey, dated 1833, placed the town on Little Uchee Creek, once called Wetumpka Creek, about 9 miles west of Phenix City and due east of Moffitt's Mill, in Lee County.[223] The town was the site of the "Green Corn Dance" celebration of the Lower Creeks. General Thomas Woodward attended a council there after the land cession of 1832 to advise the Indians to comply with the treaty.[224] Witumka's importance increased with the decline of old Kawita. After 1832 it was regarded as the leading town of the Creeks who did not remove to the West.[225]

YUFAULA (Eu-fau-lau-hatchie, Yufalahatchi, Eufaulee Old Town). This Upper Creek town was situated on the north side of Talladega Creek about 15 miles above its confluence with the Coosa River. It existed just south of Talladega, and 2 or 3 miles east of Mardisville, in Talladega County.[226] In 1799, Benjamin Hawkins stated that this town was "15 miles up the Eufaulau-hatchie, on the left side of the creek, and bordering on a branch. It is well watered and the residents have a fine stock of cattle, horses and hogs."[227]

YUFALI (Nafolee, Upper Ufala). This Upper Creek town was on the east bank of the Tallapoosa River, near the mouth of Eufaubee Creek, in Macon County.[228] During the early eighteenth century this town was inhabited by the Amissi (or Massi) tribe, a band of unknown origin. In the census of 1760, there were 100 warriors living at Yufali. Tradition states that Osceola was born near this town.[229]

YUFALI (Yufala). The remains of a number of Lower Creek towns are found along the banks of the Chattahoochee River in Houston County, including the town of Yufali, which was situated 5 miles below the mouth of Omussee Creek.[230] A band of Yamasee Indians lived among the Upper Creek Indians in this vicinity during the middle of the eighteenth century. They were possibly the same group that had lived at the mouth of Deer River, on Mobile Bay, as early as 1715. They later moved across the Chattahoochee River, eventually settling in west Florida.[231] A large domiciliary mound marks the site of a Yamasee town on Omussee Creek, some 6 miles northeast of Dothan.[232]

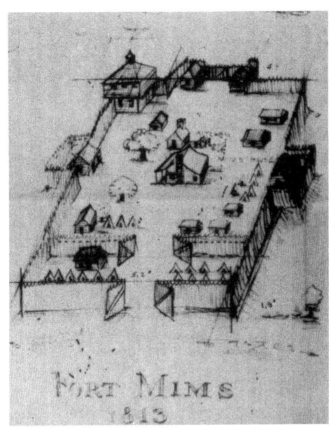

Drawing of Fort Mims, 1813, by Fletcher Hale. (Courtesy Alabama State Department of Archives and History.)

Ceremony in preparation of the removal of the remains of Governor John Sevier, of Tennessee, from the grave at Fort Decatur, Alabama, in 1888. The gentleman at the right corner of the fence is Governor Thomas Seay, of Alabama; the gentleman leaning on the left of the fence is Governor Robert L. Taylor, of Tennessee. (Courtesy Alabama State Department of Archives and History.)

VIEW U. STATES ARSENAL, MT VERNON, AL.

The United States Arsenal, Mount Vernon. (From La Tourrette's Map of Alabama, 1838.)

Geronimo, the Apache leader, when he was incarcerated at Mount Vernon Arsenal in 1888. (Courtesy Alabama State Department of Archives and History.)

In 1825, General Lafayette, of Revolutionary War fame, dedicated the new Alabama Masonic Lodge No. 3, while on a visit to Claiborne. In recent times, the building was moved to Perdue Hill.

PART II

FORT SITES

Throughout Alabama's long and colorful history many fortifications have been erected within its borders. The French colonists constructed the first fort, Fort Louis de la Mobile, in 1704 at Twenty-seven Mile Bluff, and during the remainder of the colonial period many other forts were built by soldiers and settlers from France, Spain, and England, some of which were afterwards occupied by Americans. Over a dozen defensive fortifications were erected during the Creek War of 1813–14 for the protection of settlements, for supply depots, and as offensive positions from which to launch campaigns against the Red Sticks.

During the Civil War, both Confederate and Union forces operated from fortifications within Alabama. An elaborate system of defenses was built to protect the port city of Mobile; a triple line of defenses (containing more than 150 cannon mounted along the lines) guarded against a land attack from the west. To protect the city from an attack from the upper area of the bay, defensive lines were established at Spanish Fort and Fort Blakeley, and a number of batteries were erected at the mouths of the rivers. Forts Morgan and Gaines were garrisoned to protect the entrance into the large bay.

It is not this author's purpose to present the sites and histories of the forts that still exist in Alabama, but to describe only the forts of the past.

FORT ARMSTRONG. This fort was probably on the north bank of the Coosa River, due east of Cedar Bluff and south of Highway 23, in Cherokee County.[1] Thomas McAdory Owen stated that Fort Armstrong was on the Etowah River, near the Coosa River,[2]

while the antebellum historian, Albert James Pickett, said that it
was situated on Coosahatchie Creek.³ According to tradition,
the site was used as a base of operations by the British during the
American Revolution. Fort Armstrong was erected by General
Andrew Jackson, who, when confronted by a number of prob-
lems in early 1814, was compelled to employ Cherokee Indians
to garrison the position. Because of its short existence, very few
records pertain to it.⁴

FORT BAINBRIDGE. Situated on the old Federal Road, this
small supply point was 17 miles southeast of Tuskegee, south of
Highway 80, near the Macon and Russell County boundary.⁵
After fighting against the Red Sticks in the battle of Autossee,
General John Floyd marched his Georgia troops back to the
Chattahoochee River, where they rested and waited for needed
supplies. After six weeks, in January 1814, the command, consisting of 1,300 soldiers and 400 Indian allies, moved westward
and erected Fort Bainbridge, naming it in honor of Commodore
William Bainbridge. They left their supplies at the fort under a
small guard and proceeded westward, where they met the enemy
on January 27 and won the battle of the Calebee.⁶

After the war, Captain Kendall Lewis, a former officer of the
U.S. Army, established the Lewis Tavern at this site to accommodate travelers on the Federal Road. His father-in-law, Big Warrior, was a silent partner in the venture.⁷

FORT BIBB. This fort stood by the old Federal Road, at the
present site of Pine Flat, on Highway 10, 15 miles west of Greenville, in Butler County.⁸ Early in 1818, only two years after
coming into this area, the settlers were warned that hostile Indians had been seen in the vicinity. Almost immediately, the fort
was established around the home of Captain James Saffold and
named in honor of William Wyatt Bibb, the territorial governor.⁹

In March, 1818, a war party led by the notorious Savannah
Jack made a surprise attack on the isolated cabin of William Ogle
and killed Ogle, a woman who was visiting the home, and several
children. A week later three men, including Captain James Saffold, were killed in the area.¹⁰ Volunteers, commanded by Sam

Dale, rushed to the relief of the settlers and erected Fort Dale
(see Fort Dale). Savannah Jack and his followers left the region
when the 18th U.S. Infantry and friendly Choctaw Indians came
there to patrol.[11]

FORT BLAKELEY. This dead town and fort site is in Baldwin
County at the northern end of Mobile Bay (see Blakeley in Part
III). To reach the site from Mobile, travel eastward on U.S. Highway 90 to Spanish Fort, turn left on Alabama Highway 225, go
for 4½ miles, and turn west on a graded road, which leads to the
site on the Tensaw River.[12]

In August, 1864, Admiral David Farragut won the battle of
Mobile Bay, capturing Forts Gaines and Morgan, thus gaining
control of the lower bay. However, for almost a year the Union
forces were unable to break through the land defenses that
guarded the city of Mobile.

Fort Blakeley was not a typical fortification, but was a 4-mile-
long barricade of pine logs covered with sand and mud, and
was constructed with nine lunettes, or zig-zags, in the line. The
flanks rested on the marshes of the Appalachee River. There
were 2,700 Confederate soldiers behind these lines or in advanced
rifle pits, and 35 pieces of artillery plus siege mortars, which made
the position more formidable than nearby Spanish Fort. The
Confederate commander was General St. John Liddell, a West
Pointer and veteran of the Tennessee campaigns.[13]

Ordered to capture Mobile, Union General E. R. S. Canby
led 32,000 men from Forts Gaines and Morgan on March 17,
1865, while Union Major-General Frederick Steele moved northwestward from Pensacola with 13,000 troops. The two columns
converged on Spanish Fort, where the defenders held out
against the vastly superior numbers for sixteen days (see Spanish
Fort).

On April 1, the forces under Steele arrived before Fort Blakeley with 75 wagon-loads of supplies and immediately began a
bombardment of the Confederate fort from only 1,000 yards
away, which lasted until April 8, accompanied by infantry skir-
mishes, sniper fire, and the roar of small arms fire.

On April 8, Canby secured Spanish Fort and immediately

began to shift his men northward for 3 miles to join Steele before
Fort Blakeley. By late afternoon 22,000 Union soldiers had
massed for an attack. At 5 p.m., the Union brigades rushed toward the center of the Confederate line, breaking through the
shattered abatis by the sheer power of numbers. Some of the
defenders were able to escape into the marshes, but 2,300 surrendered to the Union forces.[14]

FORT CARNEY. Erected at Gullett's Bluff, this defensive position overlooked the Tombigbee River, approximately 6 miles
below Jackson, in Clarke County.[15] The small stockade was built
in 1813 by Josiah Carney, who had come to Clarke County in
1809 from North Carolina. The Reverend T. H. Ball, who wrote
an early history of the county, stated that the fort had only a few
inhabitants. Fort Carney was abandoned early in the Creek
War when the settlers received an alarm that Red Sticks were in
the region.[16]

CATO'S FORT. A small defensive stockade, Cato's Fort was
on the west side of the Tombigbee River, about 5 miles south of
Coffeeville, and about 1 mile west of the river, near the Choctaw-
Washington County line.[17] It was erected in 1813 by settlers as a
precautionary measure but was abandoned soon after the Creek
War began.[18]

FORT CHINNABEE. This small fort stood on the north bank
of Big Shoal Creek, near the influx of Wolfskull Creek, 6 miles
east of Oxford, in Calhoun County.[19] Chinnabee, a friendly
Creek chieftain, built the fort 3 miles north of his village in 1813
(see Fort Lashley).

FORT CLAIBORNE. On a high bluff overlooking the Alabama
River, this fort was near the mouth of Limestone Creek. The site
is just off U.S. Highway 85, on the Monroe County side of the
bridge that crosses the Alabama River.[20] General Ferdinand L.
Claiborne erected the fort during the Creek War of 1813–14
as a base for supplies. The bluff on which the fort was built was
known as Alabama Heights.[21] Howell Tatum described it in

1814: "a strong built Stockade Fort nearly a square on the centre of three squares are built Blockhouses which have the effect of Salient Angles, the outer ends of which are shaped so as to have the effect of the face of Bastions in defence—there is also one of them in the line of an irregular off set in the work, made to avoid including part of a ravine."[22] Settlers began to arrive in the vicinity in 1816, and the town of Claiborne soon claimed the site of the fort (see Claiborne in Part III).

FORT CONDÉ. This famous French fort in Mobile occupied the square bounded by Theater St., St. Emanuel St., Church St., and Royal St.[23] When Bienville, the French governor, moved his colony from Twenty-seven Mile Bluff to Mobile in 1711, a square stockade was built of cedar stakes, with a bastion situated in each corner, and was called Fort Louis de la Mobile.[24] In the latter part of that same year, Crozat, the new French governor, rebuilt the fort with bricks and renamed it Fort Condé de la Mobile. The new fortification measured 300 feet between each of the corner bastions. The river was only 100 yards from the guns of the fort. Enclosed within the walls were officers' quarters, a guardhouse, two long one-story barracks, an open square, two wells, and two subterranean rooms, one housing a bakehouse and the other a powder magazine.[25]

The British obtained the fort by the terms of the Treaty of 1763 and renamed it Fort Charlotte.[26] On March 14, 1780, during the American Revolution, the fort was captured by Spanish forces under Gálvez. The Americans forced the Spaniards to surrender the fortification on April 13, 1813,[27] and the Spanish forces evacuated the fort on April 15. The Americans then garrisoned troops there until 1820, when the fort was razed and the property sold to the Mobile Lot Company.[28]

FORT CRAWFORD. This fort was situated 1 mile from Brewton, across Murder Creek, on lands that later became the site of the Downing-Shofner Industrial Institute, in Escambia County.[29] Probably Fort Crawford was established by Major-General Edmund Pendleton Gaines, some time between 1815 and 1818 on the Alabama-Spanish East Florida frontier, to halt molestation of settlers in that area by Indians. One hundred regulars of the 7th U.S. Infantry, under the command of Major White Youngs, were garrisoned there in 1818. It was abandoned before 1821.[30]

CURRY'S FORT. This fort was built on the east bank of the Tombigbee River, approximately 4 miles south of Jackson, in Clarke County.[31] Erected for the defense of settlers residing in the area, Curry's Fort was in use in 1813. Colonel James Caller stopped at the fort while leading his militiamen to Burnt Corn Creek, where they fought the first battle of the Creek War on July 25, 1813.[32]

FORT DALE. At Poplar Spring, this fort was 5½ miles north of Greenville, near U.S. Highway 31, in Butler County.[33] Colonel Sam Dale established the fort in 1818 on the old Federal Road as a defense against hostile Indians led by Savannah Jack (see Fort Bibb).[34]

FORT DECATUR. Situated on the east bank of the Tallapoosa River, this fort was near the community of Milstead, in Macon County.[35] Colonel Homer Y. Milton and his Carolina troops established the fort in March, 1814. John Sevier, the first governor of Tennessee, died at Fort Decatur on September 24, 1815, while engaged in a boundary settlement between Georgia and the Creek Nation. He was buried at the site, but his body was removed in 1888 and sent to Knoxville for reburial.[36]

FORT DEPOSIT. This supply point was at the mouth of Thompson's Creek, on the south bank of the Tennessee River, in Marshall County.[37] Andrew Jackson and the Tennessee Militia established Fort Deposit in October, 1813. Colonel John Coffee brought the spoils of war, 300 bushels of corn that he had captured at Black Warrior's Town, to be stored at this position before the militia proceeded into the Creek Nation.[38]

FORT DEPOSIT. This fort was on the site of the present community of that same name, in Lowndes County.[39] While marching to destroy the Red Stick village of Ikanatchaka in December,

1813, General Ferdinand L. Claiborne established this fort as a place to deposit his military stores and to set up a field hospital. It was guarded by 100 men.[40] The Federal Road ran by the site, and later Fort Deposit was used as a position of safety by the settlers in the area.

FORT EASLEY. The site of Fort Easley was on Wood's Bluff, on the east side of the Tombigbee River, in Clarke County.[41] Erected in 1813 as a defensive position for the settlers residing in the area, it was on a flat area about 100 yards above the river landing, where the bluff is almost perpendicular, and where a spring offered the inmates fresh water. It enclosed about 3 acres.[42]

A "love feast" or camp meeting was held there in August, 1813, just outside of the walls. Guards were stationed around those attending the religious meeting to prevent a surprise attack.[43] Shortly after this event, news came informing the inhabitants of the fall of Fort Mims (August 30, 1813), and Fort Easley was quickly evacuated because of the crisis.

GLASS REDOUBT. This small fort was situated just south of Suggsville near the Alabama River, in Clarke County.[44] In July, 1813, Zachariah Glass built the fort as a defensive position for settlers residing in the area. The redoubt was evacuated shortly after the Kimball-James Massacre, and the inmates flocked to Fort Madison, which was only 225 yards away (see Fort Madison).[45]

FORT GULLETT (Gullett's Bluff). This small Confederate fortification was on the Tombigbee River about 4 miles south of Jackson, in Clarke County.[46] Said to have been on the site of a pioneer fort, Fort Gullett was built in 1862 to guard the nearby salt works from Union raids. It was abandoned during the last months of the war.[47]

FORT HAMPTON. On the Elk River, at the present site of Harmony Church, this early fort was 17 miles west of Athens on Highway 72, in Limestone County.[48] Colonel Reuben J. Meigs,

U.S. Army, established the fort in 1809 to keep squatters off Indian lands. He named it in honor of General Wade Hampton, his superior officer, who was at the time stationed in Huntsville. Meigs's cavalry was kept busy attempting to drive the squatters from the area, and while carrying out their duties, the military force built a road to Huntsville. Fort Hampton was abandoned in 1817 after the Indians ceded the area to the U.S. Government.[49]

FORT HULL. This fort was erected on the old Federal Road (U.S. Highway 80, 5 miles southeast of Tuskegee, in Macon County.[50] During the winter of 1813–14 Georgians under the command of General John Floyd built the fort. After the battle of Calebee, the militiamen made a retrograde movement back to Fort Hull, leaving the Red Sticks in possession of the battlefield (February 2, 1814). Soon afterwards, fearing that an attack would soon be launched against Fort Mitchell, Floyd marched with the bulk of his army to Fort Mitchell, leaving but a small detachment to guard Fort Hull.[51]

FORT JACKSON. The site of this fort is between the Coosa and Tallapoosa rivers, just off Highway 231, about 5 miles south of Wetumpka, in Elmore County.[52] After breaking the power of the Red Sticks at the battle of Horseshoe Bend, General Andrew Jackson marched his men to the ancient site of Fort Toulouse where they erected Fort Jackson (see Fort Toulouse). The men first cleaned out the old trenches and then built a stockade and blockhouses.[53]

William Weatherford, the victor at Fort Mims, surrendered there to General Jackson in April, 1814. On August 9, the Red Sticks signed the Treaty of Fort Jackson, giving up much of their former tribal lands.[54] Soldiers remained stationed at the fort after the conclusion of the Creek War, and settlers held court there until May, 1818. Thereafter it was abandoned and fell into decay as had Fort Toulouse.

LANDRUM'S FORT. In the Good Springs Beat (Section 18, Township 8, Range 2 East), this fort was 11 miles west of Fort

Sinquefield, in Clarke County.[55] Landrum's Fort was one of several forts erected in Clarke County by the settlers during the Creek War of 1813–14.

FORT LASHLEY. Several log buildings have been reconstructed at this site, which is on Fort Lashley Avenue across from the former Deaf School for Negroes, in the city of Talladega.[56] Alexander Leslie, Jr., built the fort in the latter part of 1813, so some early records refer to it as Fort Leslie. Leslie's father had come to the Creek Nation as a Tory during the American Revolution and had served as the secretary of the chieftain, Alexander McGillivray. Selocta Chinnabee and Jim Fite, two Creeks, helped build the fortification, a defensive position for Creeks who refused to join the Red Sticks (see Talatigi in Part I).[57]

Davy Crockett, who came to the fort with Jackson to fight against the Red Sticks who lay siege to the fort, wrote that a branch "ran partly around the fort." He also stated that a platform was built around the inside of the palisades, which was designed as a stand for soldiers who could fire over the top of the palisades.[58]

FORT LAVIER. The Clarke County historian, Rev. T. H. Ball, believed that the fort was southeast of Suggsville, in Clarke County, although the exact site is uncertain.[59] This fort was probably built shortly before the fall of Fort Mims and was erected around the residence of Captain Lawson Lavier. Soon after the Kimball-James Massacre (September 1, 1813), the fort was abandoned by the inmates who rushed to Fort Madison for safety.[60]

FORT LOUIS DE LA MOBILE (Fort Louis de la Louisiana). This fort was on the west bank of the Mobile River, 27 miles north of Mobile Bay, near Mount Vernon, in Mobile County.[61] Realizing that the Mississippi coast was not the most appropriate area for a French colony, Iberville, a young French-Canadian war hero, received permission to move his colony to the Mobile River. However, because of Iberville's illness, his twenty-two-year-old brother, Bienville, was chosen to supervise the removal. Thus

Bienville erected the fort and city on the banks of the Mobile River in early 1702.[62] Although the official name of the colony was Fort Louis de la Mobile, it was commonly called Twenty-seven Mile Bluff. The purpose of the French colony was to establish trade with the Indians, so the town was not at first surrounded by walls. The fort was built as a precautionary measure against raids by other Europeans. The erection of the fort began in January, 1702. Jean Penicaut, a soldier-author, first visited the installation on March 18, 1702, and found the fort in excellent condition. It was a square structure, built of logs, with a bastion in each corner containing 6 cannon each. Within the fort were a large parade ground, a church, officers' quarters, and a guardhouse. Barracks for the soldiers were 150 paces up the river. A brick powder magazine, 24 feet square by 10 feet deep, was also located outside of the fort along the river bank.[63] A severe flood struck the town in March, 1711, and soon afterwards Bienville decided to abandon the position and move to the site of Mobile.[64]

MCGREW'S FORT. Situated near the Tombigbee River, this small fort was 3 miles north of old St. Stephens (Section 1, Township 7, Range 1 West), in Clarke County.[65] Two brothers, William and John McGrew, built this palisaded fort, which enclosed an area of 2 acres, as a defensive position against the Red Sticks in 1813.[66] Colonel William McGrew was killed in September in an ambush near Bashi.[67]

FORT MADISON. This fort was near the Alabama River, 1½ miles west of Suggsville, in Clarke County.[68] Settlers built this defensive fort some 225 yards north of Glass Redoubt in August, 1813, and enclosed one acre of land (60 yards square). Just outside of the 12-foot-high walls was a trench 3 feet deep. Portholes were cut in the walls for the use of sharpshooters inside. At night pitch pine was burned on scaffolds to illuminate the area outside the walls.[69]

Soldiers, who had been sent to Glass Redoubt by General Ferdinand L. Claiborne, aided in the construction of Fort Madison.[70] After the attack on Fort Sinquefield on September 3, 1813, the settlers from Sinquefield, Glass, and Lavier rushed to Fort Madison for more security.[71] Unfortunately, depredations in the vicinity caused Claiborne to move 200 soldiers and 500 settlers from the fort to St. Stephens, creating consternation among the settlers who remained in the fort. However, Captain Sam Dale and Captain Evan Austill soon arrived with 80 militiamen for protection.[72] Claiborne later retracted his former order and returned soldiers to Fort Madison.

FORT MIMS. This famous fort was near Boatyard Lake (Section 5, Range 2 East, Township 2 North), just west of Alabama Highway 59, in the Tensaw-Montgomery Hill area of Baldwin County, approximately 12 miles north of Stockton.[73] In the summer of 1813, settlers of this area built a stockade around the home of Samuel Mims, an old Indian countryman who operated a ferry on the Alabama River. The square fort enclosed an acre of ground and had large gates on the eastern and western sides. A number of buildings were within the fort, including Mims's house, a loomhouse, and several hastily erected cabins. A blockhouse was started but never completed.[74] Albert James Pickett, the antebellum historian, stated that 553 people, including 265 soldiers, were within the fort at the time of the fatal battle. A large number of the settlers were "half-breeds" with relatives who belonged to the Red Sticks.[75]

In July, 1813, General Ferdinand Claiborne had sent Major Daniel Beasley to command the fort. Dixon Bailey, a local half-breed, was elected captain. On August 7, Claiborne inspected the position and instructed Beasley to "strengthen the pickets and to build one or two additional blockhouses," but that order was never accomplished.[76]

On Monday, August 30, one thousand warriors, under the command of William Weatherford, the "Red Eagle," rushed through the open gate at noon. The battle lasted from two to three hours within the fort. Only about 36 whites survived, and settlers began to cry out "Massacre!," and "Remember Fort Mims!" A burial party came to the burned-over site on September 9, and dug trenches for the dead.[77]

In 1955, members of the Till family donated the 5-acre site to the State of Alabama.[78] The site was placed in the National Register of Historic Places in September, 1972.[79] The Alabama Historical Commission, in 1973, donated a large grant for excavations to be made in the area by a competent archaeologist.

FORT MITCHELL. The site of this fort is in the community of the same name, on Alabama Highway 165, a few miles south of Phenix City, ½ mile from the Chattahoochee River, in Russell County.[80] The fort was erected by General John Floyd during the Creek War in 1813 and was named in honor of David B. Mitchell, the governor of Georgia.[81] Late in 1817, the Creek Indian Agency was established at the fort with John Crowell as agent.[82]

In 1825, the famous Revolutionary War hero, the Marquis de Lafayette, visited Fort Mitchell while on a tour of the South and was entertained by the Indians, who performed in one of their thrilling ballgames.[83]

Several famous duels were fought at or near this fort. George W. Crawford, a national figure, shot and killed Thomas Burnside there in 1828.[84] A Major Camp killed General Woolfolk at the fort in 1832.[85]

By the terms of the Treaty of 1832, the Creeks ceded 18,000 acres of their tribal lands to the U.S. Government and moved to the Indian Territory (Oklahoma). After this time the Agency ceased to exist, and the buildings became a part of Crowell's private property.

FORT MONTGOMERY. Situated just opposite the "Cut Off" of the Alabama River, the fort was 2 miles from the site of Fort Mims, in Baldwin County.[86] Thomas McAdory Owen believed that this fort was erected in 1814 by Lieutenant-Colonel Thomas H. Benton for use as a supply base.[87] However, the antebellum historian, Albert James Pickett, stated that a burial party from this fort was sent to the site of the Kimball-James Massacre in September, 1813.[88]

MOUNT VERNON CANTONMENT AND ARSENAL. The remains of this cantonment and arsenal are on the grounds of

Searcy Hospital at Mount Vernon, just off U.S. Highway 43, 30 miles north of Mobile, in northern Mobile County. Established in December, 1811, by Colonel Thomas Cushing, this fortification was designed to avoid an international dispute between the American settlers and the Spanish authorities in Mobile.[89] During the Creek War of 1813–14, this cantonment was the headquarters of General Ferdinand L. Claiborne. After the fall of Fort Mims, hundreds of refugees flocked to the safety of this position.

An act of Congress, approved on May 24, 1828, established a U.S. arsenal there,[90] which was garrisoned by federal troops until 1861, when it was seized by the Alabama Militia under the orders of Governor Andrew B. Moore. Confederate forces occupied the position until the close of the Civil War.

United States troops converted the arsenal into barracks in 1873 and garrisoned the position until 1890. When the great Apache leader Geronimo and his band of Chiricahuas surrendered in 1886, they were exiled to prisons in Florida, where their numbers were seriously decreased by disease. The Indian Rights Association pressured the government to remove the survivors to Mount Vernon, where they were promptly transferred. Seven hundred Apaches, including Geronimo, were held as prisoners at this site from 1886 to 1893, where they were allowed to live outside the post in log cabins and to farm.[91]

In 1895, the military property was signed over to the State of Alabama, and the Legislature, on December 11, 1900, placed the property in the hands of the newly created Mount Vernon Hospital, now Searcy Hospital.[92]

FORT OKFUSKEE. On the Tallapoosa River, at the Indian village of Okfuskee, this fort was 40 miles northeast of the site of Fort Toulouse.[93] Fearing French competition in the Creek Nation, British traders erected the fort around 1735. They were able to hold the support of some of the Upper Creeks, but on the whole the venture was unsuccessful. After only a few years Fort Okfuskee was abandoned.[94]

FORT PIERCE. This small fort was 2 miles southeast of Fort

Mims, in Baldwin County.[95] John and William Pierce erected the fort early in 1813. On the day of the Fort Mims massacre, August 30, 1813, the settlers within Fort Pierce trembled with terror as they heard the gunfire, but were totally unable to go to the aid of their neighbors. When the Red Sticks did not attack this position, the inmates abandoned the fort and fled to Mount Vernon.[96] Fort Pierce remained unoccupied until November, when General Claiborne placed Lieutenant-Colonel George Henry Nixon there.[97]

FORT POWELL. This Confederate fort was on a sandbar just north of Heron Island, 2 miles north of Dauphin Island, near the mouth of Mobile Bay.[98] The Confederate Corps of Engineers built the fort to guard the shipping lane (now known as Grant Pass) between the mainland of Alabama and Dauphin Island. On August 4, 1864, during the battle of Mobile Bay, Union Admiral David Farragut ordered the *Chickasaw*, under Lieutenant-Commander George H. Perkins, to shell Fort Powell. On the following night, after withstanding a heavy shelling, the Confederates escaped to the mainland, blowing up the fort behind them.[99]

FORT ST. STEPHENS. The site of this famous fort and town is on the west bank of the Tombigbee River, approximately 9 miles from Leroy, near St. Stephens in Washington County (see St. Stephens in Part III).[100] The Spaniards first erected a fort there in 1789 to guard against American encroachment and to conciliate the Indians living in that region. In 1791, the commandant of the fort was Captain Fernando Lisoro. His home, a Catholic church, and blockhouses were considered to be the finest buildings at the post, and were constructed of framework and plaster. There were also a number of inferior buildings, which were small and crudely covered with bark.[101]

In 1799, the fort and town were turned over to the American authorities, when it was learned that the property lay on the American side of the boundary. Lieutenant John McClary and soldiers of the 2nd U.S. Infantry, after marching from Natchez, took possession of the site on May 5, 1799.[102]

In 1805, George Strother Gaines stated that the former

Spanish fort "was located on the bluff by the river; one of the block-houses was in a good state of preservation and was occupied as the store. There was an extensive war-house, a room which was used as the land office; and a frame dwelling, which had been the officer's quarters, all enclosed on three sides with pickets and a ditch, the river forming the defenses on the fourth."[103]

When the Red Sticks went on the warpath in 1813, the inhabitants of the town erected Fort Republic, a position considered to be impregnable by the Creeks. At that site in September, 1813, the great Choctaw chieftain, Pushmataha, offered his services to the Americans.[104]

SAND FORT. On the old Federal Road, this small fort was 10 miles west of Fort Mitchell, and 6 miles northwest of Seale, in Russell County.[105] Sand Fort, so named because it consisted of an earthwork of sand, was built by General John Floyd and his Georgia Militia in 1814 as a rendezvous point for his men.[106] In 1836, a storekeeper was held in his house by a guard of hostile Indians in the vicinity, and on learning of this act, settlers in the area once again used Sand Fort as a defensive position but abandoned it before the end of the year.[107]

FORT SINQUEFIELD. This fort was on the west bank of Bassett's Creek (Section 13, Township 8, Range 3 East), approximately 5 miles southeast of Grove Hill, in Clarke County. The spring that supplied the inmates with water is in a valley some 275 yards southwest of the fort site. Unmarked graves are 90 feet northwest of the site.[108]

During the Creek War settlers in the vicinity erected this defensive fort, which was said to have been smaller than Fort Madison.[109] After the massacre at Fort Mims, settlers flocked to Fort Sinquefield for safety, so the fort became overcrowded and conditions within became almost unbearable. Because of these conditions, the families of Ransom Kimball and Abner James chose to return to Kimball's large cabin, which was only a mile from the fort. On September 1, 1813, Red Sticks attacked the cabin without warning, killing 13 women and children. Six survivors escaped to the fort.[110]

That night the inhabitants of the fort stood guard for fear of

an attack. It was raining, so it was impossible to hear any un-
usual sounds in the forest surrounding the fort. Mrs. Sarah Mer-
rill, the daughter of Abner James, had been scalped and left for
dead in the smoldering ruins of the Kimball cabin. She was revived by the rain, and crawled among the bodies of her relatives
and friends, to look for her baby. After finding the infant alive,
she staggered to Fort Sinquefield.

On September 3, soldiers from Glass Redoubt were sent to
the Kimball home, where they recovered the bodies and returned to Sinquefield with them in an oxcart. Graves were
opened approximately 90 feet outside the walls of the fort, and as
the burial services were being conducted, Josiah Francis and 100
Red Sticks attempted to ambush the mourners and several
women who were washing clothes in the nearby creek. The
mourners were able to reach the fort safely, but the women were
surrounded. One woman was killed. Isaac Hayden, on horseback
and leading a pack of hounds, rushed into the Red Stick band and
saved the lives of the other women.

The Red Sticks then rushed for the gate of the fort, losing at
least 20 warriors to the guns of the 35 defenders. The surviving
Indians then retreated from the field of battle into the forest.
The inmates of the fort, fearing an even larger attack by Weatherford and his 1,000 warriors, abandoned the position and hur-
ried to the safety of Fort Madison.[111]

SPANISH FORT. The site of this fort can be seen in the resi-
dential area of the town of Spanish Fort, just off U.S. Highway
90, on the eastern shore at the northern section of Mobile Bay,
in Baldwin County. During the American Revolution, Spanish
troops, under the leadership of Bernardo de Gálvez, captured the
port city of Mobile from the British. Mobile then became the
Spanish base of operations to act against the British capital at
Pensacola (the capital of British West Florida). But instead of
attacking immediately, Gálvez spent a year in preparation. It
was at this time that the Spanish fort was constructed on the
eastern side of Mobile Bay.[112]

Before Gálvez could began his offensive against Pensacola,
the British made their move. On January 3, 1781, British Gen-

eral John Campbell ordered Captain Von Hanxleden to attack Spanish Fort. On January 7, the officer was killed while engaged in a bayonet attack on the fort, and his men retreated to Pensacola. In May, Gálvez captured the British capital on the Gulf.[113]

Eighty years later, Confederates established a defensive position on the site of the old Spanish Fort to guard the approach to Mobile in the upper bay region. Three redoubts, connected by rifle pits and backed up by artillery, stretched across an area some 2,500 yards long, running from the Appalachee River to Bayou Minette. At the time of the battle there in 1865, General Randall Gibson was in command with 2,500 men. On March 27, 1865, Union General E. R. S. Canby, with 32,000 men, lay siege on the position. The number of Confederates fell to 1,800, when a unit was sent back to Blakeley.

For fourteen days the gallant defenders held out against all odds. Canby began his final assault on April 8, blasting away at the Confederate front with 90 cannon while Union gunboats battered the rear. Finally, under the cover of darkness, the defenders spiked their cannon, then slipped into the marshes, where they waded out to boats that had been brought from Mobile for the evacuation. The following morning the Union army marched into the empty position (see Fort Blakeley).[114]

FORT STODDERT. The site of this fort is on the west bank of the Mobile River, approximately 4 miles south of the junction of the Alabama and Tombigbee rivers, and 2½ miles east of Mount Vernon, in Mobile County.[115] Named in honor of Secretary of the Navy Benjamin Stoddert, the fort was erected in 1799 by Captain Bartholomew Schaumburgh, of the 2nd U.S. Infantry.[116] It was a typical fort of that period, with palisaded walls and a blockhouse in each of the four corners.

In February, 1807, Aaron Burr was held at Fort Stoddert for a few days after being arrested by Captain Edmund P. Gaines, the commander of the fort. He was housed in the commander's home and became a close friend of the family.[117]

Alabama's first newspaper, the *Centinel,* was published at Fort Stoddert. The first issue was printed on May 23, 1811.[118]

In July, 1813, General Ferdinald L. Claiborne, fearing trouble from the Red Sticks, marched with his Mississippi militiamen to this fort, where he immediately distributed troops to the defensive stockades that were being erected by the settlers. Soon afterwards, Claiborne established his headquarters at Mount Vernon Cantonment, and Fort Stoddert was abandoned.[119]

FORT STROTHER. On the west bank of the Coosa River, this site is 4 miles west of Ohatchee, opposite the mouth of Charchee Creek, in St. Clair County.[120] General Andrew Jackson erected Fort Strother in 1813, just before the battle of Talladega. It enclosed an area of approximately 100 yards, and contained a blockhouse in each of the four corners. Inside the fort were a supply building, 8 huts used as a hospital, and 25 tents. A hundred hogs were kept inside to keep them safe from the Indians.[121]

SULPHUR BRANCH TRESTLE FORT. Situated on a mountaintop near Sulphur Springs Creek, this fort was in the vicinity of Elkmont, 8 miles north of Athens, in Limestone County.[122] The Union forces built the fort in order to guard a major trestle on the Alabama and Tennessee Railroad. The earthen fortification was garrisoned by the 9th and 10th Indiana Cavalry. There were two large blockhouses on the site.

The Confederate "Wizard of the Saddle," General Nathan B. Forrest, after capturing the Union garrison at Athens, accepted the theory that federal soldiers would soon be sent from Tennessee to Corinth, Mississippi via this railroad. He hastened to destroy all trestles and bridges along the line, the most important of which was Sulphur Branch Trestle.[123]

On the morning of September 25, 1864, Forrest drove in the Union pickets, then placed his artillery in a position from which he delivered a deadly bombardment into the fort. Soon afterwards, the Union commander, Colonel Lathrop, was killed along with 200 of his men. The Confederates then rushed the fort, and Colonel J. B. Minnis, offering no resistance, surrendered 973 men, 700 stands of arms, 300 horses, 2 pieces of artillery, and other supplies.[124] On entering the fort, a private in Forrest's 7th Tennessee Cavalry stated: "I saw no more horrid spectacle during the war than the one which the interior of that fort presented. If a cyclone had struck the place, the damage could hardly have been worse."[125] On September 29, Forrest moved northward to destroy other bridges, after sending the prisoners southward to the Tennessee River.

FORT TOMBÉCBEE (Fort York, Fort Confederation). This fort was situated on Jones' Bluff, on the west side of the Tombigbee River, several hundred yards north of the bridge on Highway 11, near the town of Epes, in Sumter County.[126] In 1735 De Lusser, on the orders from Governor Bienville, built the fort to serve as a base from which the French and the Choctaws would attack the Chickasaws and the British. The fort measured 173 feet on the side by the river, 304 feet on the creek or south side, 231 feet on the north side, and 278 feet on the west side. Ten-foot walls enclosed approximately one acre. Within was officers' quarters, a guardhouse, barracks, an interpreter's apartment, storehouses, and a granary. Outside the walls stood a house built to accommodate visiting Indians.[127]

The French occupied the fort until they were forced out of America by the terms of the Treaty of Paris of 1763, and on November 22, 1763, British Lieutenant Thomas Ford took possession of the structures, renaming it Fort York.[128] Leaving an Indian agent there to trade with the Choctaws, British troops abandoned the position in 1766. Even the agent moved out during the cold winter of 1768, ending the British occupation there.[129]

In 1815, George Strother Gaines visited the site while searching for a place to erect a trading post. He found many of the old pickets still standing, but all of the interior buildings were gone. One hundred yards away he found the home of a settler, Samuel Jones, who claimed that the home was built by the French in the olden times.[130] Gaines, with the aid of 13 soldiers, hired carpenters to complete a trading post on the site in May, 1816. At this post a group of commissioners met with the Choctaw chiefs in October, 1817, and signed a treaty by which the Indians agreed to give up their tribal lands on the eastern side of the Tombigbee, an agreement that brought hundreds of settlers into the region.[131]

FORT TOULOUSE (Aux Alibamos). This fort was on the east
bank of the Coosa River, approximately 1 mile from its junction
with the Tallapoosa River. The site lies 5 miles south of Wetumpka,
near U.S. Highway 231, in Elmore County.[132] Embittered against
the British because of the Yamasee War of 1715–16, the Creek
Indians invited the French to erect a trading post in the Alibamo
country (the Alibamos were part of the Creek Nation).[133] Thus,
in July, 1717, Lieutenant La Tour selected this site on a large
bluff overlooking the Coosa River and only 500 yards from a
bend in the Tallapoosa River.[134]

Named in honor of the Count of Toulouse, the log stockade
was approximately 100 yards square, with 4 bastions, each containing 2 cannon. The stockade had 3 gates, and a moat encircled
the walls. On the side of the fort facing the Coosa was a watch-
tower. Frame buildings housed the officers and men. A brick
powder magazine held explosives, guns, and other supplies.[135]

Fort Toulouse was a trading post for the Creek Indians and a
military position only in relation to the infringing British. An
Alibamo village was within "musket shot" of the fort, and many
other Indian villages were in the vicinity. Because of the dullness
of the duty there, a mutiny occurred only four years after
the fort was erected, and the commandant, Marchand, was
killed. In 1733, Bienville hired Swiss mercenaries to help fill the
garrison.[136]

During the French and Indian War (1754–1763), the French
strengthened the installation, with a total of 50 soldiers stationed
there. After losing the war in 1763, Chevalier Lavnoue, the
commandant, spiked the cannon, destroyed much of the property, and abandoned the position. British troops occupied the
fort for a short time, then they too abandoned it.[137]

When General Andrew Jackson arrived on the site in 1814, he
found only a ruin in the wilderness and on the site erected Fort
Jackson (see Fort Jackson). The site is today the property of the
State Department of Archives and History and is being developed
as a tourist attraction.[138]

TURNER'S FORT. This defensive stockade was near the
northwestern bend of the Tombigbee River, in the West Bend

neighborhood, in Clarke County.[139] In 1813, the pioneers living in northwestern Clarke County built this small fort at the residence of Abner Turner as a defensive position against the Red Sticks. It was constructed of split pine logs, which were doubled for thickness. There were 2 or 3 blockhouses on the site.[140] In this fort 13 men and boys guarded the women and children of the community. Among the inmates was the heroic Tandy Walker, who had earlier saved Mrs. Crawley from the Red Sticks at Black Warrior's Town. Early in September, 1813, the settlers evacuated the position and fled to the safety of St. Stephens.[141]

FORT TYLER. Situated on the west bank of the Chattahoochee River, this small Confederate fort was 2 miles west of West Point, Georgia, and just east of Lanett, in Chambers County.[142] In 1865, fearing that Union raiders would attempt to capture West Point, Georgia, Confederate General Robert Charles Tyler crossed the Chattahoochee River and erected Fort Tyler, "a strong bastioned earthwork, 35 yards square, surrounded by a ditch 12 feet wide and 10 feet deep, situated on a commanding eminence." Two 32-pounders and 2 field guns were mounted behind the abatis.[143] At 10 a.m., April 16, 1865, Union Colonel O. H. LaGrange, with a large detachment of Wilson's Raiders, attacked the fort and captured the position, after 7 of his men were killed and 32 wounded. General Tyler was killed along with 18 of his brave defenders.[144]

FORT WHITE. This small defensive fort was a short distance northeast of Grove Hill, in Clarke County.[145] Very little information is available concerning the history of this position. When General Ferdinand L. Claiborne and his Mississippi Militia reached Mount Vernon on July 30, 1813, he learned that this fort and several others had been erected by settlers as defenses against Red Stick raids.[146] It was probably abandoned soon after the fall of Fort Mims.

FORT WILLIAMS. This site is now inundated by the waters of the Coosa River. It was at the mouth of Cedar Creek, near the community of Talladega Springs, in southwestern Talladega

County.[147] Early in March, 1814, General Andrew Jackson sent Colonel Williams, of the 39th Regiment, down the Coosa River from Fort Strother with the supplies for a third campaign. Jackson then spent five days cutting a road to the mouth of Cedar Creek, where he joined Williams and built a fort, naming it in honor of his fellow officer, on March 22.[148]

Several days later, leaving a small detachment at the fort to guard the supplies, Jackson and his army marched against the Red Sticks, fighting the battle of Horseshoe Bend on March 27. He arrived back at Fort Williams on April 2 with his wounded (54 of his men had been killed in the battle and 156 wounded). Many of the wounded died there and were buried near the fort.[149]

The Old Academy, at Cahaba, as it appeared at the time of its dismantling in 1902–03. After the buildings of the former capital city were razed, the bricks were loaded onto steamboats and shipped to Mobile and to towns along the Alabama River. (Courtesy Alabama State Department of Archives and History.)

A business block on the south side of Vine Street, Cahaba, just prior to its dismantling in 1902–03. (Courtesy Alabama State Department of Archives and History.)

The Kirkpatrick Mansion as it appeared at the turn of the century. This fine old home was built in Cahaba by "Shoestring" Barker in 1857, and burned in 1935, the last of the once proud mansions of the former county seat. (Courtesy Alabama State Department of Archives and History.)

The 26-room mansion of the "merchant prince of Cahaba," Edward M. Perine, resembled a baronial castle. It was razed at the turn of the century. (Courtesy Alabama State Department of Archives and History.)

Cedarwood, the oldest home in Hale County, was built in 1818 by Joseph Blodget Stickney on land purchased from General Charles Desounettes Lefebvre, lands originally belonging to the Vine and Olive Colony. It was moved to Havana in 1975 by Edward P. Whatley, Jr., who plans to restore it.

The James Dellet House, built around 1816, is the last remaining mansion in Claiborne, once a cotton shipping center on the Alabama River. It now belongs to Mr. and Mrs. W. E. Deer.

PART III

COLONIAL, TERRITORIAL, AND STATE TOWNS

Many historic towns and villages of the past are today but vague memories, and they can be described only by those who study the dusty records, the annals of Alabama. The names of most of these dead towns have disappeared from modern maps, while only a few names of rural communities mark some sites. Only vine-covered brickbats and broken fragments of glass remain as relics of many of these once-populated centers of civilization, and some are now covered by forest.

To students of history, who are often romantically inclined, the terms "dead town" or "ghost town" conjure up more than images of long-abandoned and decaying buildings, weed-covered streets, and lichen-covered tombstones; their active imaginations can recreate the laughter and sadness of a bygone age; to them the streets are no longer just empty depressions in the wilderness, but are once again busy thoroughfares of travel and trade; ancient foundations once again support houses and businesses; the long-forgotten cemeteries are emptied and their inhabitants are resurrected and again are active participants in life.

The purpose of this section is to conjure up a sampling of the ghosts of Alabama's past, to give their approximate sites, and to record a few brief highlights of their histories. Most of the towns here listed have disappeared completely, but a few remain on modern maps although they have lost their former importance and have become but shells of the past.

AIGLEVILLE (Eagleville). This early French village was 1 mile east of Demopolis, which is today within the boundaries of that city, in Marengo County.[1] After Napoleon had been defeated at Waterloo and forced into exile on St. Helena, 30,000 of his former followers left France and sailed to America. The United States Congress, on March 3, 1817, granted to a group of these exiles 92,160 acres of land near the confluence of the Black Warrior and Tombigbee rivers, for a price of only 2 dollars per acre.[2]

Under the leadership of General Count Charles Lefebvre Desnouettes, these exiles sailed from Philadelphia to Mobile and were transported to the "White Bluff," where they founded Demopolis, the "city of the people." Quickly and crudely they erected cabins, cleared land, and attempted to cultivate the grape and olive. However, they had little agricultural knowledge, and the plants that had been shipped to them from Europe were either dead or dying and had little chance for survival.[3] To add to their misery, the settlers discovered that Demopolis lay outside their claim, and they were forced to abandon the site, which was quickly claimed by the Americans. Thus, with downcast eyes and aching hearts, the French men and women moved a mile to the east and founded the village of Aigleville.[4]

A report, dated December 12, 1821, from Agent Villar at Aigleville to the Secretary of the United States Treasury stated that 81 "cultivators of the soil" had farmed 1,100 acres and 327 inhabitants lived there. Each of the settlers was assigned a lot in the village, a vegetable plot nearby, and farming land in the vicinity.[5] But many of the inhabitants soon became dissatisfied and moved away to Arcola, or north to Hale County, or south to the city of Mobile (see Arcola).

After the death of Napoleon, most of the exiles were pardoned and returned to France. General Desnouettes also sailed for Europe but was drowned when the ship on which he traveled sank off the coast of Ireland.[6] Aigleville existed as late as 1828, but by 1848 no signs remained of the people from France.[7]

ALABAMA CITY. This early town was on the eastern shore of Mobile Bay, on the site now occupied by Fairhope, in Baldwin County. During the early 1830s, large ocean-going ships were barred from sailing to the port of Mobile by a large sandbar extending from the mouth of Dog River, and businessmen found it expensive to transfer cargoes to light draught boats, therefore Alabama City was founded as a port on the other side of the bay. The town first appeared on a state map in 1838, located on the Bay Shore Road, between the towns of Blakeley and Williamsburg. For a short time it posed a threat to the commerce of Mobile, but became unimportant when the Panic of 1837 ruined its principal backers. It continued to be on state maps until the early 1880s, but had disappeared in 1895 when Fairhope was established on the site.[8]

AMERICA. This small Walker County community was between the towns of Cordova and Parrish. A post office was established at this site on January 19, 1891. At the time the town was part of a community known as Hewitt. On December 23, 1895, the name of the community was changed to America. The post office was finally closed and discontinued on April 30, 1956.[9]

ARBACOOCHEE. This gold-mining center was situated just north of Dime Creek, 9 miles southeast of Heflin, in Cleburne County. Gold was first discovered in East Alabama about the year 1830. The triangular gold belt covered an area approximately 3,500 square miles within the state. The so-called Arbacoochee Gold District was between the Georgia line and the Talladega Mountains and contained alluvial deposits, which consisted of free nuggets and gold flakes mixed with sand, gravel, and dirt.[10]

The town of Arbacoochee was founded in the mid 1830s in the center of the Arbacoochee Gold District and was rapidly occupied by gold-hungry miners with dreams of "striking it rich." By 1845, the town had a population of 5,000, and shacks and tents were erected on every available spot of ground. Arbacoochee also had 2 churches, a school, 20 general mercantile stores, 5 saloons, 2 mining equipment stores, 2 hotels, a fire department, a racetrack, and over 100 permanent homes.[11]

The gold boom continued until 1849, when news arrived that gold had been discovered in California. Residents rushed to the more promising western gold fields, and the town was almost abandoned. A few miners remained until the outbreak of the

Civil War, when operations at the Dahlonega (Georgia) Mint ended.[12]

ARCOLA. The site of this "Vine and Olive" town is on the south bank of the Black Warrior River, a mile northeast of the mouth of Yellow Creek, approximately 4½ miles northeast of Demopolis, in Marengo County.[13] Arcola was first established by the French Bonapartists (see Aigleville),[14] but was soon used as a river landing by the planters living in the vicinity.

During the Annual Convention of the Episcopal Church, which met in Tuscaloosa in 1832, the Reverend Albert A. Muller stated that official acts had been performed during the year "in the village of Arcola." In 1843, he reported two baptisms and one funeral at the Arcola mission. Again, in 1844, the mission was briefly mentioned, but it never again appeared in the church records after that year.[15]

ASHFORD SPRINGS. This popular watering place was situated in the eastern half of the southeast quarter of Section 15, Township 15, Range 2 West, in Choctaw County.[16] The famous springs were once the favorite resort of wealthy planters of Choctaw and Sumter counties. One of the springs contained white sulphur, another sulphur-chalybeate, and another vichy. Today nothing remains of the resort except a marble basin at one of the springs.[17]

BAINBRIDGE. Situated on the south bank of the Tennessee River, this early town was 6 miles east of Florence, in Lauderdale County. An overgrown cemetery is all that remains today of Bainbridge, once a popular river crossing. When settlers first rushed into the Tennessee River Valley just before 1819, they had dreams of establishing a great commercial city at the Muscle Shoals. Land promoters grew wealthy as they sold off lots at high prices in the town of Bainbridge, and citizens erected large homes and several substantial brick stores.[18]

On January 16, 1819, the commissioners of the town issued a report stating that Bainbridge was laid out on an inclined plain "so that the streets when filled will resemble the seats of a theatre."[19] They boasted that the water supply was excellent, with

Hawkins' Creek and 20 springs as the source. A ferry operating on the site could cross the Tennessee River in eight to nine minutes.[20]

A great rivalry existed between Bainbridge and nearby Melton's Bluff, the county's first seat of justice (see Melton's Bluff). While Andrew Jackson, the future President, and his associates backed the settlement of Melton's Bluff, the Reverend Turner Saunders and John Donelson sought to prove that Bainbridge was on a more promising site.[21]

The building of a railroad from Tuscumbia to Decatur settled the issue when it bypassed Bainbridge. By 1840, merchants had begun an exodus to the more favorable towns of Tuscumbia and Florence. The number of inhabitants rapidly dwindled, the ferry ceased operations, and Bainbridge became a ghost town.[22]

BELLEFONTE. The site of this town was 1½ miles from Hollywood, just northeast of the Tennessee River, approximately 14 miles southwest of Stevenson, in Jackson County. On December 13, 1821, Jackson County commissioners selected the infant town of Bellefonte, which was situated on the principal stage road through North Alabama, as the county seat.[23] Incorporated earlier in the year, the town had a population of approximately 200 people. The courthouse was constructed in 1828, and soon the town contained 6 mercantile stores, a drugstore, a blacksmith shop, a tavern, a church, a Masonic hall, and an academy.

Bellefonte remained the county seat until 1859, when the county offices were removed to Scottsboro. During the Civil War, Union troops destroyed the former courthouse. By 1869 most of the citizens had abandoned the town and moved their businesses to nearby Hollywood, a town on the Southern Railway.[24] In 1870, Bellefonte contained only 72 inhabitants.

BENNETTSVILLE. This small town and road junction was 1 mile north of Attalla, and 10 miles north of Gadsden, in Etowah County. Appearing at the junction of a road leading northward to Fort Deposit on the Tennessee River and a road from Ashville to the Coosa River at Brown's Ferry, Bennettsville was first on the state map in 1838.[25] It died when Attalla, founded in 1870, became an industrial town on the railroad only a mile away.[26] It was last listed on a map in 1874.

BIBB COURT HOUSE (Bibbville). An early county seat, this town was in Section 29, Township 23 North, Range 11 East, approximately halfway between Centreville and Randolph, in Bibb County. Settlers began to migrate into this area in 1815. The Falls of the Cahawba, the site of present-day Centreville, was designated as the temporary county seat, and commissioners were appointed to select a permanent site. The commissioners were slow to make a selection and apathetic in their deliberations, so an election was held in February, 1828, and the people of the county chose Bibb Court House over the Falls of the Cahawba as the county seat.[27] The date of the removal of the county offices to Centreville is now unknown. However, Bibb Court House disappeared from the state map in the latter 1830s.

BIRMINGHAM. Situated on the banks of Coon Creek, in Coon Valley, this village was 4 miles west of Stevenson, in Jackson County. Never incorporated, Birmingham was created on December 29, 1845, when a post office was established for the community, which boasted of its attractive homes and farms, a store, churches, a coal mine, and a tannery. The Nashville and Chattanooga Railroad did not come down the valley as had been anticipated but was constructed through nearby Crow Creek Valley, so the community began to decline rapidly after the Civil War.[28]

BLADON SPRINGS. The site of this once famous watering place is on Alabama Highway 31, 3 miles west of the Tombigbee River, in southeastern Choctaw County. Early settlers in this area recognized the curative properties of the six springs there. In 1838, James Conner, the owner of the springs, opened the area to the general public, and it soon became the "Saratoga of the South." The Bladon Springs Hotel, which could accommodate 200 guests, was opened in 1846, and a village was founded near the hotel grounds where many wealthy families erected permanent homes. During the late summer, visitors thronged into the area from all over Alabama, Mississippi, and Louisiana.[29]

The resort remained open during the Civil War years, but visitors had to "rough it." In the early period of Reconstruction, Negro troops, commanded by white officers, were allowed to terrorize the inhabitants in the area and many crimes resulted.[30]

For the remaining three decades of the nineteenth century the hotel and resort were in full operation. The resort declined as the automobile developed into a means of reaching the seashore and mountain retreats, and the hotel fell below its former standards. Finally, a lumber concern leased the building for the use of logging crews, and in 1934 the State purchased the property and converted it into a park. Only 7 families were living in the area when the hotel was destroyed by fire in 1938. Today the hotel and cottages are gone, and only occasional visitors come to the once popular area.[31]

BLAKELEY. The site of this one-time rival of Mobile can be found at the northern end of Mobile Bay, in Baldwin County. To reach the site from Mobile, travel eastward on U.S. Highway 90 to Spanish Fort, turn left on Alabama Highway 225, travel for 4½ miles, and then turn westward on a graded road to the Tensaw River.

Josiah Blakeley, a native of Connecticut, came to the Spanish city of Mobile in 1806. In 1807, he took the Spanish oath of allegiance and purchased three islands in the upper reaches of Mobile Bay, containing a total of 12,000 acres. On one of these islands he established his home, Festino Plantation, where he raised cattle and cultivated rice.[32]

Blakeley then purchased White House Plantation, which was situated at the point where Bayou Salome empties into the Tensaw River, from Dr. Joseph Chastang. In May, 1813, he employed James Magoffin, a surveyor, to lay off a town there, hoping to establish a port city that would rival Mobile. The town was laid out with two public squares. The streets that ran in one direction were named for famous men, and those running in the opposite direction were named for trees, flowers, and shrubs.[33]

Land speculators from Mobile invested in the town, and on January 6, 1814, the town was incorporated.[34] Blakeley died in

1815, but his town continued to thrive, having a population of
several thousand people in 1820.

An advertisement, published in 1817, stated:
"The town of Blakeley is regularly laid out, with streets 99 feet
wide, running at right angles, east and west, north and south.
It is situated upon two general benches of land;—the one in front
on the river is 25 feet in height above tide-water; then about one
quarter of a mile back the ground rises gradually for half a mile,
till it gains an elevation above the level of the sea of one hundred
feet—thence a beautiful plain for nearly a mile, when the land
rises into a ridge of two hundred and fifty feet above high water
mark.

"No town in the United States is better supplied with fresh
water, than Blakeley. A great multitude of never-failing copious
springs of the purest water issue from the high table of land within the plat of the town, as well as from the high ridge in its rear.
. . . The numerous groves of majestic live oaks, interspersed over
the site of Blakeley, will with judicious reservations of such as
fall within the streets, not only become a great ornament to the
town, but be a source of much comfort to the inhabitants during
the influence of an almost vertical sun. This promising town is
rapidly improving. Some of the principal merchants at Mobile,
and also several mercantile merchants from New York, Boston,
New Orleans, and elsewhere, have recently purchased lots of the
original proprietors, and are now erecting suitable warehouses,
stores, and dwelling houses in Blakeley, preparatory to extensive
business there in the fall. There is, at present, a great competition
between the proprietors of Blakeley and Mobile. Which town is
to take the lead in trade is at present unknown. . . ."[35]

On December 22, 1818, the merchants of Blakeley petitioned
the United States Congress for the privilege of becoming "a Port
of Entry and Delivery." The petition stated that the town had a
"spacious, convenient, and secure" harbor, with 23 merchants
operating 16 different establishments, with merchandise con-
signed to commercial business exceeding a half million dollars.[36]

The Blakeley Sun, a weekly newspaper, was established in the
town in 1819,[37] the same year that John Motley opened the Blake-

ley Hotel and Boarding House. A ferry made the run to Mobile and back each day.[38]

Severe yellow fever epidemics struck the town in 1822, 1826, and 1828. Many deaths occurred as a result of the coastal plague, and the epidemics, coupled with the high prices demanded by the land speculators, brought about the rapid demise of the town. Most of the citizens abandoned the town and moved to Mobile before the Civil War, and Blakeley was a ghost town at the time of the battle there (see Fort Blakeley in Part II).[39]

BLUFF CITY (Monroe). Situated on the south bank of the Tennessee River, this town was 4 miles north of Somerville, in Morgan County. In 1818, Monroe was shown on a territorial map,[40] and a year later it was mentioned in legal records when Moses Harlan was authorized to operate a mill there. Soon afterwards, Thomas D. Crabb established one of the first ferries in what was then called Cotaco County near the town.[41] Postal records indicate that the town was still called Monroe between 1852 and 1857. The post office was discontinued after 1857 but reopened in 1874 as Bluff City. This post office closed its doors forever in 1881 when the river traffic abandoned the town in favor of the more modern facilities at the landing in Decatur.[42]

BOOTSVILLE. This small village was situated in Sand Valley near the foot of Sand Mountain, in De Kalb County. Named for an Indian chief who had once lived there, this temporary county seat never became large enough to appear on a state map. The courthouse there was only a crude log structure. Surviving only a few years, Bootsville lost its settlers who moved away to nearby Camden, a village near Portersville.[43]

BRIDGEWATER. An antebellum river landing, Bridgewater was on the east bank in a bend of the Elk River, approximately 8 miles northwest of Athens, in Limestone County. It was listed on a map of the Northern District of the Alabama Territory in 1817,[44] and last appeared on the state map in 1850.

BRUNSON. Situated between the Pea River and White Water Creek, this small village was approximately 10 miles northeast of Elba, in Coffee County. Very little information exists about the village. A school opened there in 1870. However, the site did not appear on a state map until 1879. John F. Brunson was appointed as the first and only postmaster there on March 30, 1898. State maps omitted Brunson early in the twentieth century.[45]

BURLESON. The site of this town is on Big Bear Creek, 5 miles west of the town of Red Bay and 17 miles southwest of Russellville, in Franklin County. A post office was established there on August 22, 1848. It was discontinued on July 18, 1866, but was reopened on June 7, 1867.[46] Captain Isaac J. Rogers, a Confederate veteran, moved to the small town in 1881 and established a general mercantile business and became one of the leading citizens of the community. He died in 1908, after selling the business to his son, John William Rogers, in 1898. In 1907, the younger Rogers closed the store and moved a few miles away.[47] The Burleson post office ceased operations on April 30, 1909, and the town became a ghost town.[48]

CAHABA (Cahawba). To reach the site of Alabama's first state capital, travel 5 miles southeast from Selma on Alabama Highway 22, turn left on a dirt road (there is a historical marker at the turn), and drive for approximately 4 miles to the Alabama River. At the territorial capital, St. Stephens, on February 13, 1818, a commission was formed to select a site for the future state capital. The site selected was at the point where the Cahaba River flowed into the Alabama River in Dallas County. The site was approved on November 21, and Huntsville was to serve as a temporary capital while the new site was being developed.[49]

In October, 1819, Governor William Wyatt Bibb reported that the town had been laid out and that lots were to be auctioned off to the highest bidders. The town was designed on the same plan as the city of Philadelphia, with streets running north and south named for trees, and streets running east and west named in honor of famous men.[50]

The first Capitol was a large, two-story, brick structure, which was 58 feet long and 40 feet wide.[51] By 1820, two newspapers were published in the town. Many stores, doctors' and lawyers' offices, and churches stood on the tree-lined streets. Many styles of residences could be found in the town, from log cabins to brick mansions. The large, two-story Bell Tavern and private boarding houses catered to the legislators and visitors.

A devastating flood of the Cahaba River struck the capital in 1825, causing a portion of the capitol to tumble down. Partisan politics entered the picture, and at the session of the legislature held in January, 1826, the motion was made, argued, and carried to remove the capital to Tuscaloosa.[52]

The sudden removal of the state facilities did not destroy Cahaba for it was still the county seat of wealthy Dallas County and a leading cotton-shipping point. During the early 1830s, several large warehouses were erected for cotton storage, and prosperity returned to the town. Businesses, schools, and churches flourished, and wealthy planters erected palatial mansions on spacious grounds, ornamented with beautiful shrubs and trees and overflowing fountains.[53]

The Civil War sounded the death knell for old Cahaba. Young gallants rushed off to "follow the flag." In 1863, a prison for captured Union soldiers, which was called Castle Morgan, was established within the town and by October, 1864, contained 2,151 prisoners.[54] But the war was lost, and a society that was based on slave labor was destroyed.

Another devastating flood struck the town in the spring of 1865, and the combination of war, flood, and the destruction of the economy brought a rapid decline to the town. And then on December 14, the county seat was removed to nearby Selma, taking with it a majority of the inhabitants.[55] Just before the turn of the century, a former slave purchased most of the town site for $500, and the abandoned homes and buildings were razed for building materials and transported by steamboats to Selma and Mobile.[56]

CAHABA OLD TOWN (Old Cahawba). This small village was situated at the junction of Old Town Creek and the Cahaba River, in Perry County. By the Treaty of Fort Jackson, dated August

9, 1814, the Creek Indians ceded a large portion of their lands to the United States. This event opened Perry County for settlement; although illegally, a number of Creeks continued to live at the mouth of Old Town Creek in a village they called Cahaba Old Town, vacating it soon after the arrival of the first pioneers.[57]

Anderson West, the first known Perry County pioneer, arrived in December, 1816, and erected his cabin near the Indian village. Soon other pioneers pushed into the wilderness, coming from the Carolinas, Tennessee, Georgia, and Virginia, to settle in the vicinity of West. William Ford and his sons erected a cabin on Perry Ridge, where they constructed a sawmill and a gristmill. Thomas M. Oliver and John Durden built a cotton gin near the old Indian town.[58]

On February 5, 1822, seven commissioners were selected to choose a permanent site for the county seat. Cahaba Old Town, Perry Ridge, Burrough's Bottom, and Muckle's Ridge were placed in nomination. After several ballotings, Muckle's Ridge (later called Marion) won, and Cahaba Old Town lost its chance of becoming the county seat. Soon it lapsed into nothing more than part of a large cotton plantation.[59]

CAMBRIDGE. Situated on the west bank of Piney Creek, this small village was approximately 5 miles southeast of Athens, in Limestone County. Very little is known about Cambridge. It first appeared on a map of the Northern District of the Alabama Territory in 1817,[60] and was last listed on a state map in 1850.

CANDY'S LANDING. This early Greene (now Hale) County landing was situated on the east bank of the Black Warrior River ½ mile north of old Lock No. 5, or 25 miles upriver from Demopolis and an equal distance south of Erie. Jason Candy established the landing about 1820.[61] It was quite popular in the early days but was unfortunately on ground subject to flooding. During the flood of 1833 the landing was reported to have been under six feet of water.[62]

Harvey Tindell acquired the landing in 1848. He was also the owner of Wheeling Landing (Tindell's Landing), which was approximately 5 miles to the north.[63] Isaac Snedecor did not mention the landing in his *Greene County Directory* in 1855, although many very large plantations were in the area, nor did it appear on a map after 1850. However, in February, 1868, the landing was mentioned in the *Alabama Beacon* as the residence of T. B. Lipscomb, who had just died there.[64]

CANTON BLUFF (Canton). The site of this early county seat was on a bluff on the west bank of the Alabama River near the community of Canton Bend, a few miles east of Miller's Ferry, in Wilcox County. Canton Bluff became the temporary county seat of Wilcox County and a voting station in 1819. In 1832, the county seat was moved to Barboursville, a town that was renamed Camden in 1841. Canton Bluff then became only one of a number of steamboat landings in the county.[65] A large brick two-story house, which is now uninhabited, is said to have been the first courthouse.

CARROLLSVILLE. This early Jefferson County village was on the Tuscaloosa Road (now called Jefferson Avenue), in the section of Birmingham now known as Powderly, near the grounds of the Belcher Lumber Company. Jefferson County was formed by the Alabama Legislature on December 13, 1819, and the first regular term of the circuit court was held at Carrollsville in 1820. The area around Carrollsville was originally settled in 1819 by the families of Joseph Hickman, William Pullin, John Brown, and William Brooks. The first school in the county was founded in this village by Thomas Carroll, a schoolmaster from York District, South Carolina. Some claim that the village was named in honor of the schoolmaster, while others state that it was named in honor of General Andrew Jackson's Inspector-General, William Carroll.[66] In 1821, the county seat was moved to nearby Elyton. However, Carrollsville continued in existence for another twenty years, last appearing on the state map in 1842.[67]

CENTREVILLE. Situated 5 miles south of the Tennessee River, this early town was on a branch of Flint Creek, in Morgan County. Centreville was one of the first towns organized in what was then Cotaco County, and appeared on the territorial map in 1817.[68] In 1818, William Johnston was licensed to operate a tavern there. The Cotaco County Court issued an order in 1819 to construct a road from "Senterville" to Crabb's Ferry on the Tennessee River.[69] The town was last listed on the Rhea Survey Map of Tennessee in 1830.

CHAMBERS COURT HOUSE. This early county seat was 3½ miles northeast of Lafayette, in Chambers County. The Alabama Legislature created Chambers County on December 18, 1832, on lands previously held by the Creek Indians, which had been ceded to the federal government at Cusseta on March 24, 1832. Judge James Thompson was elected to the county court of Chambers and chose the home of Captain Baxter Taylor as the temporary county seat. Around this home grew the village of Chambers Court House, which was situated on the Chapman Trail, an important road of the period.[70]

On April 20, 1833, the first meeting of the Circuit Court was held in the Taylor home, and because the village had no hotels, Captain Taylor served food at moderate prices to visitors. Three commissioners were elected to find a proper site for a permanent county seat, and they selected Lafayette near the center of the county. Lots were sold there in late October, 1833, bringing the end to the old seat.[71]

CHANDLER SPRINGS. The site of this once famous resort may be found on Alabama Highway 77, approximately 10 miles southeast of the city of Talladega, in Talladega County. James Chandler, a tailor from Texas, established his home at the springs in 1832. Several years later he was granted 500 acres at the site, where he built a two-and-a-half-story hotel and a quadrangle of log cottages with a dance pavilion.[72] A post office was installed here in 1838, which was called Mountain Springs. In 1844 the office was renamed Maria Forge, and in 1855 it became Chandler Springs.[73]

The resort became famous nationally after the Civil War. Wealthy families erected private cottages on lands purchased in the vicinity. After Chandler's death, the property went through several hands. Finally, in 1918, the hotel burned to the ground and cottages were razed. Only one cottage remains on the site.[74]

CHULAFINNEE. This gold-mining town was situated on the south bank of Chulafinnee Creek, 12 miles south of Heflin, in Cleburne County. It was 7 miles southwest of the gold-mining town of Arbacoochee. Chulafinnee, in the Arbacoochee Gold District, came into existence in 1835, and during its boom years was only half the size of Arbacoochee. It is stated that Chulafinnee was a more permanent type of town than its rival because of the number of brick buildings there.[75]

Tradition states that the King brothers, of the family that later founded the famous King Ranch in Texas, were prospectors there. Before leaving the town to serve in the Confederate army, a King was said to have destroyed the mine field with dynamite.[76] It was last listed on the state map in 1878.

CLAIBORNE. The site of this old town is on the east bank of the Alabama River, in the rural community of Claiborne, on U.S. Highway 84, 12 miles west of Monroeville, in Monroe County. Settlers moved to Fort Claiborne, situated on the river bluff, shortly after the termination of the Creek Indian War of 1813–14, and erected their cabins in the vicinity (see Fort Claiborne in Part II).[77]

In 1817, an advertisement stated: "At fort Claiborne, on the Alabama river, 100 miles from Mobile by land, and 40 miles east of St. Stephens, a considerable village has been made since the war, where there is a brisk retail trade to the settlement in its vicinity. It lies on the east side of the river on very elevated ground, called the Alabama heights."[78]

The town was surveyed under the orders of General John Coffee in 1819, the lots were numbered, and land sales soon began. The state incorporated the town on December 20, 1820. The following year Justus Wyman wrote: "The town stands on a high bluff of land called the Alabama Heights, about 180 feet above the level of the river. The first settlement commenced in this town towards the close of the year 1816; since that time it has increased with a rapidity scarcely paralleled. The whole number of inhabitants which one year ago did not exceed 800, is now rising of 2,000. . . . The houses are merely of a temporary nature, built of logs, and put up for present use only . . . ."[79]

Many cotton plantations were on both sides of the river in the vicinity. A large warehouse for the storage of cotton was erected on top of the bluff, and the heavy bales could be pushed down a covered slide to the wharf below. The *Harriet* was the first steamboat to reach the landing (1821),[80] and afterwards the town became a regular landing for the river traffic.

In April, 1825, the Revolutionary War hero, General Lafayette, visited the town during his tour of the South. He was entertained in the new Masonic Lodge, which originally stood on top of the bluff, but which was later moved to Perdue Hill, where it may be seen today.[81]

In 1830, Claiborne contained two large hotels—the Washington Hall and the Claiborne Hotel—many stores and business houses, a cotton warehouse, a boarding house, a jail, churches, and many fine residences.[82] Claiborne remained an important shipping point and trading center throughout the antebellum years and Civil War period, but after the war the economy of many cotton planters in the area had been destroyed. By 1872 the town contained only 350 persons.[83] Families gradually moved away to Mobile and other cities. Today the rural community contains one store, a few small homes, and one old mansion (built by James Dellet, a lawyer).

CLARKESVILLE. Approximately 8 miles west of Grove Hill, this early county seat was just north of Tattilaba Creek, in Clarke County. On December 13, 1819, the Alabama Legislature appointed a group of commissioners "to select and fix on the most suitable site for the seat of justice, in and for the county of Clarke; having due regard to health, water, and accommodations; provided such seat shall not exceed 3 miles from its center."[84] On December 7, 1820, the Legislature declared that this county seat was Clarkesville, so the first courthouse was erected there.[85]

Dissatisfaction over the site of the county seat caused the legislature, on January 15, 1831, to make provisions for a change. An election was held in April, 1831, for commissioners to select the new site. The site chosen was Macon, which was later re-named Grove Hill.[86] Clarkesville became just another rural town and disappeared from the map entirely during the last quarter of the nineteenth century.

CLAYSVILLE. This village was just to the north of a big bend in the Tennessee River, across from Guntersville, in Marshall County. The Alabama Legislature created Marshall County on January 9, 1836. Popular election chose the small village of Claysville as the first county seat. In 1838, the seat was removed to the town of Marshall, to Warrenton in 1841, and to Gunters-ville in 1848.[87] Claysville remained on the state map until the early 1900s.

COLBERT'S FERRY. The Colbert family claim and ferry were situated at the point where the Natchez Trace (now the Natchez Trace Parkway) crossed the Tennessee River, in Colbert County. George Colbert was born in the Chickasaw Nation around 1764, the son of a Scottish trader and Chickasaw mother. When the Federal Government began to construct the Natchez Trace (between Nashville and Natchez), the Chickasaws were given the right to establish ferries within their Nation to serve the famous road. Colbert established his ferry across the Tennessee River at the mouth of Bear Creek between 1797 and 1800.[88] While the ferry was being constructed, United States soldiers were stationed on the south bank of the river, where they erected a building and built a ferryboat.

The ferry was quite profitable for Colbert, who soon became the wealthiest man in the Nation and was able to purchase many additional slaves for his plantation. The building constructed by the soldiers was given to Colbert as soon as the road was completed, and he converted it into a refreshment and supply stand for travelers.[89]

Colbert's Ferry continued in operation until 1819 or 1820, when a road was opened through the town of Florence and took away the trade. George Colbert then moved to another part of the Chickasaw Nation (in the vicinity of Tupelo, Mississippi), where he purchased two plantations, which he operated with the labor of 140 slaves.[90]

COTTON PORT. The site of this early landing was just south of the town of Mooresville, on the northern bank of the Tennessee River near Piney Creek, in Limestone County. In 1808, Benjamin French established his pioneer home on Limestone Creek, but soon removed to the site of the future Cotton Port. A short while later the first cotton was shipped from Limestone County to New Orleans, and Cotton Port became an important landing. Business houses and warehouses were erected. A man named Higgins built a large two-story residence in 1818, the first brick edifice in the county. Prosperity was short-lived for the early landing. By 1819, the planters found it more convenient to ship their products from Brown's Ferry. Cotton Port continued to be listed on the state maps, last appearing in 1850.

DITTO'S LANDING (Whitesburg). Situated on the north bank of the Tennessee River, this early Madison County river landing was 10 miles south of Huntsville, approximately where U.S. Highway 231 crosses the river today. John Ditto, a Pennsylvanian, was possibly the first white man to reside in what is today Madison County. He operated an Indian trading station long before the settlers came into the region. He established the first landing used by the pioneers between Chattanooga and Colbert's Ferry.[91]

In 1820, John Hardie operated a store at Ditto's Landing, where he received and distributed goods for the firm of Read and White (see Mardisville). Colonel James White, who owned an ironworks and a salt firm in East Tennessee, shipped his products to Hardie by way of the river. Hardie wrote to his brother on May 8, 1820: " . . . from this place all the cotton made in this [Madison County] is shipped to New Orleans, in flat bottomed boats each conveying from 250 to 350 bales; the whole quantity sent from here will consist of from 15 to 17,000 bales each wg.

about 300 lbs."[92] By the summer of 1825, Ditto's Landing had been renamed Whitesburg in honor of Colonel White.

DUDLEYVILLE. This small town was 14 miles west of Lafayette and approximately 12 miles south of the Horseshoe Bend battle site, in Tallapoosa County. Johnson Jones Hooper, the humorist who lived at Lafayette, visited Dudleyville while practicing law between 1835 and 1840.[93] The town did not appear on a state map until 1842.[94]

The body of Major Lemuel P. Montgomery, who had fallen at the battle of Horseshoe Bend in 1814, was reinterred at Dudleyville in June, 1839, during a reunion of Creek War veterans, and buried in a new coffin in front of the Hall McIntosh home, across the street from the post office.[95]

The town was abandoned during the early years of the twentieth century. In April, 1972, the body of the war hero was removed with ceremony to the Horseshoe Bend National Park.[96]

DUMFRIES. This early landing was situated on the west bank of the Tombigbee River, just north of the mouth of Bilboa Creek, approximately 18 miles south of old St. Stephens, in Washington County. This forgotten landing appeared on Lucas' map of Alabama in 1819, on the road between St. Stephens and Mobile. It last appeared on a state map in 1839.

ELYTON. The heart of this early county seat was its courthouse, which stood at the approximate site of Elyton School, at 100 Tuscaloosa Avenue, in western Birmingham, in Jefferson County. William H. Ely, of Hartford, Connecticut, a commissioner of the Connecticut Asylum for the Deaf and Dumb, an institution supported entirely by charity, received a federal grant for a township of land in Alabama, in March, 1819. Early in 1820, he came to the newly formed state to select his township, which would be divided and sold at auction for the charitable organization. While in the pioneer village of Frog Level, he deeded to Jefferson County a large lot for a courthouse and jail, and in appreciation the local citizens renamed the village Elyton. It was incorporated by the State Legislature on December 20, 1820.[97]

On the road between Huntsville and Tuscaloosa, Elyton soon became a trading center and stagecoach stop. In 1821, Elyton became the county seat (see Carrollsville). A two-story, brick courthouse was constructed, and a school was established.[98]

Elyton had a tavern that served as a hotel as early as 1820 and was the temporary residence of William H. Ely.[99] Joseph Hickman sold his Jefferson County farm in 1854 and operated a tavern-hotel in the town for four years before moving to Pickens County.[100]

Religion came to the town in 1818, when the pioneer Methodist minister, Ebenezer Hearn, established a log "preaching house" there. This building was later replaced by a frame building, known as the Elyton Methodist Church (now the Walker Memorial Methodist Church).[101]

The town continued to thrive during the latter part of the antebellum period. Judge William S. Mudd built a beautiful home known as Arlington, which is today a landmark of Birmingham. The *Jones Valley Times*, a weekly newspaper, began publication in 1854,[102] and the *Elyton Alabamian* came out in 1860.[103]

On June 15, 1861, the Jefferson County Volunteers were organized at Enon Camp Ground in Elyton, and soon became Company B, 10th Alabama Regiment, C.S.A. Alburto Martin, an Elyton attorney, was elected captain and led this company in many Virginia engagements.[104]

In March, 1865, Union General James H. Wilson led 13,500 cavalrymen on a raid through North Alabama, the final objective being the ironworks and arsenal at Selma. At Elyton, the General established his headquarters at Arlington, from which he dispatched General Croxton with a detachment to Tuscaloosa, where they destroyed the University and other public buildings. Other raiders were sent out to destroy the pig-iron furnaces in Jefferson and surrounding counties.[105]

After the close of the war Elyton once again conducted county business. The death knell tolled for Elyton when the railroad came to the nearby, newly formed city of Birmingham in 1871. The courthouse was destroyed by fire in 1870, and was rebuilt in the new industrial "Magic City" in 1873.[106]

Some may not believe that Elyton should be included in a volume of ghost towns, because the area is today a part of the largest city in Alabama. It is agreed that Elyton did not disappear as had Cahaba, St. Stephens, or Claiborne, but as an independent city it did not survive.

ERIE. The site of a former county seat of Greene County is located on a high bluff overlooking the Black Warrior River, on the farm of Charles O. Parkel, approximately 4 miles southwest of Sawyerville, and 13 miles west of Greensboro, in Hale County. When Greene County was established in 1819, Erie was chosen as the county seat. Greene County at that time consisted of what is today Greene and Hale counties. A courthouse was soon after constructed, and the town was incorporated on December 18, 1820.[107]

Religion was first brought to Erie by the Reverend James Monette, a Methodist, who had preached his first sermon in the county in 1818. He came to Erie in 1819,[108] making it his home, and died there on March 23, 1834.[109]

Advertisements from early Greene County newspapers contain information about the early merchants of the town. James C. Pharis and Franklin Robinson conducted business there as early as 1823, and D. W. Edgerly had a dry goods store there in 1824. Because the town was an important cotton-shipping point on the river, James T. Torbert erected a large warehouse there around 1823. Jacob Cribbs published a newspaper in 1830, which lasted for three years.[110]

In 1838, the voters of the county chose to move the county seat to Eutaw. Arguments in favor of removal were that Erie was not centrally located, that roads in the area were almost impassable during the rainy season, and that the town had a poor supply of drinking water.[111] After the removal of the county seat, the town began to decline slowly. Many of the prominent business and social leaders moved to Eutaw or to Greensboro, but even then the town continued to serve as a shipping point. In November, 1849, James T. May advertised that he had erected a new warehouse, and stated that "Erie is the only landing on the Black Warrior that is not subject to flooding."[112]

Before the building of the new warehouse, it was announced (July 29, 1848) that the Erie post office had been discontinued.[113] The town appeared for the last time on state maps in 1850. In 1855, Snedecor, in his *Greene County Directory,* wrote that Erie's "glory has departed. . . . and now a few dilapidated tenements, the ruins of the old courthouse and jail, one old homestead and its hospitable occupants. . . . are all that are left to bear witness that Erie ever rejoiced in a prosperous existence."[114]

FAIRFIELD. This early Pickens County landing was on the west bank of the Tombigbee River, 1 mile west of Cochrane. Very little has been recorded about this former steamboat landing. Nelson F. Smith, the antebellum Pickens County historian, stated that it was not yet in existence in 1831.[115] It was first listed on a state map in 1842, and Smith wrote that it was a flourishing landing and place of business by 1856.[116] Shortly after the Civil War the railroad bypassed the town and the inhabitants moved to the tracks, 1 mile to the east, where they established the town of Cochrane.[117]

FALL CREEK. Situated at the head of Fall Creek, near the Cullman-Morgan county line, this small village was in the northeast quarter of Section 36, Township 8 South, Range 2 West, in Cullman County. A post office was established at this village on November 27, 1891. Thomas J. Evans was the only person to serve as postmaster there. The office was closed on November 30, 1904.[118]

FALLS CITY. This village was in the southeastern corner of Winston County, 15 miles north of Jasper. The site now lies below the waters of Lewis Smith Lake. During the 1820s, the Davis-Randall gang of counterfeiters established their headquarters in a cave behind the waterfall on Clear Creek. After members of the gang passed counterfeit bills in Tuscaloosa, a posse traced them to the cave, captured them without a fight, and returned with them to Tuscaloosa where they were tried and soon after executed.[119]

Over the years a small village slowly was formed at the falls, and on September 29, 1853 a post office was established in the village, which was known as Clear Creek Falls.[120] One of the first of two Methodist churches in the county was erected there, and the Baptists established Bethlehem Church in the community.[121]

Life moved at a slow pace in the village until the 1880s, when the lumbering and coal businesses produced a slight boom. On March 30, 1888, the name of the village was changed to Elk, and on February 15, 1908, it was changed to Falls City.[122]

During the depression of the early 1930s, the owners of much of the local property realized that the land had become only a tax burden, therefore they sold it to the United States Forest Service. The families moved away from the area, and the post office was closed on November 30, 1953. In 1956, a civic-minded Jasper physician, Dr. W. R. Snow, sought to have the area around the falls developed as a tourist attraction, but his dream failed to materialize when the Alabama Power Company acquired the site as part of the Lewis Smith Lake lands.[123]

FILLMORE. This small town was situated on the eastern bank of Cedar Creek, just above the point of confluence with Murder Creek, in Escambia County. Named in honor of President Millard Fillmore, this town first appeared on a state map in 1853, on the road from Sparta (the county seat, which was 15 miles to the north) to Milton, Florida.[124] The Alabama and Florida Railroad, constructed just before the Civil War, bypassed the town, so business there declined. It was omitted from state maps after 1878.

FORT DALE. For the site and early history of this town, see Fort Bibb in Part II. Butler County was created by the Alabama Legislature on December 13, 1819. Commissioners appointed to select a county seat chose Fort Dale as the site. The first county election was held there on December 13, 1819, at the home of Jesse Womack. In December of the following year, the county

seat was removed to Buttsville (now Greenville).[125] Fort Dale
continued to be included on state maps, being shown at an important road junction, but it disappeared by the mid 1860s.

FRANKLIN. Situated on the west bank of the Chattahoochee
River across from Fort Gaines, Georgia, this landing was 4 miles
north of Shorterville, in Henry County. The river landing first
appeared on state maps in 1838, at a junction of a road leading
westward to Abbeville and a road leading northward to Tuskegee.[126] A map in 1874 showed a railroad crossing the river at this
site, between Cuthbert, Georgia, and Abbeville.[127] Franklin disappeared from the map at the turn of the century.

GLENNVILLE. This old-time cultural and educational center
of East Alabama was 17 miles north of Eufaula and 8 miles south
of Seale, in Russell County. Glennville was named in honor of
one of its first settlers, the Reverend James E. Glenn, a native of
Franklin County, North Carolina, who came to the area in late
1835, with two other gentlemen. A short time later they established the village of Glennville, which soon consisted of a blacksmith shop, a cobbler's shop, and a gristmill.[128]

In 1836, the Creek Indians made a bold effort to retain their
lands in eastern Alabama. Receiving an early warning that the
Indians were on their way to attack the village, and with no fort
to ensure their safety, the settlers abandoned their possessions
and fled across the Chattahoochee to Georgia. Only one citizen
lost his life, Major William Flournoy, who was killed as he left
his cabin on Hatchechubbee Creek. The Indians destroyed the
village, along with Glenn's cabin and Methodist meetinghouse.[129]
The Indian attack did not destroy the soul of Glennville, but
brought about a rebirth and an increase in population and importance. The Creeks were forced to give up their lands to the
pioneers. Glenn returned with the other inhabitants and remained in the community until his death in March, 1851.[130]

During the antebellum years Glennville contained Methodist
and Baptist churches, a hotel, a Masonic Hall, stores, and
numerous homes along the shady streets. Mansions, such as the
Glennville Plantation, were built in the vicinity.[131] Male and
female academies were incorporated by the Alabama Legislature

on January 27, 1846. The Glennville Female College was incorporated on February 10, 1852. It was the successor to an earlier school founded in 1851. This college was destroyed by fire in 1865.[132]

In 1860, the male academy became the Glennville Male Collegiate and Military Institute. The Confederate legislature of the state appropriated $150,000 to operate the school to train young men for Confederate service. Operations ceased in 1865, and the two-story building was destroyed by fire in the late 1870s.[133]

On February 7, 1854, the Glennville Railroad Company was incorporated to bring business to the cultural center. However, many of the families were against the industrialization of the town. While debates were taking place, the Mobile and Girard Railroad was routed through nearby Fort Mitchell, so eventually Glennville began to decline.[134]

GOLDVILLE. A former Tallapoosa County boom town, Goldville was northeast of Alexander City, a mile or so from the point where Alabama Highway 49 crosses into Clay County. Prospectors and alluvial gold miners rushed into this area during the early 1830s, coming mainly from Georgia. A number of productive mines were established in the area, such as the Goldville, Hog Mountain, Ely Pits, Birdsong, Log Pits, and Dutch Bend mines.[135]

Soon the town of Goldville became the mining and trading center of the district. By the middle of the 1840s, the town was composed of 12 stores, a hotel, a school, several churches, 3 barrooms, a mining supply store, and a racetrack for the "sporting gents." At the height of the boom over 3,000 were said to have lived in the town in either permanent dwellings or in 2 large tent camps. Until 1840, most of the gold seekers used the alluvial method of mining, but after that time ore mines were sunk into the hilly region and a water-powered crushing mill was installed. Ore from the Hog Mountain site ran in excess of one hundred dollars a ton.[136]

In 1849, news of the great California gold rush reached Alabama and hundreds of the Goldville miners departed for the "Golden West." Goldville continued to exist through the 1930s, but it had become a mere shadow of its former self. After the standard United States rate for gold fell to $35 per ounce, gold mining was hardly worthwhile in Alabama, but with a much higher rate today, the venture may be worthwhile once more.[137]

GOSHEN. This small town was 3 miles southeast of Coloma and 12 miles northeast of Jacksonville, in Cherokee County. Little is known about Goshen. It was first listed on a state map in 1856, on the road from Center to Jacksonville. Four years later another road made a junction here, from Georgia to Turkeytown. It last appeared on the map in 1878.

GUMPOND. Situated on or near the present boundary of Winston and Lawrence counties, Gumpond was just north of the Grayson community of Winston County. Very limited information can be found concerning this now forgotten village. A post office was established there on June 18, 1877, and remained in existence until September 30, 1914.[138]

HAMPTON RIDGE. An early county seat of Conecuh County, Hampton Ridge was situated on a hill just west of Murder Creek, approximately 10 miles south of Bellville. Samuel Buchanan is thought to have been the first settler in Conecuh County. In 1815, he built a cabin on what later became Hawthorne's Mill Creek. A short time later, Alexander Autrey settled on the creek which bears his name but removed to a line of hills west of Murder Creek in 1816. He gave the name "Hampton Ridge" to one of the hills, which was occupied a few months later by a number of families.[139]

From the time of its founding, Hampton Ridge grew rapidly and became the county seat in a close race over its chief rival, Bellville. The courthouse was a crude, one-room, chestnut-log structure, in which a rough table stood on a floor of packed dirt. Because there was no jail in the town, prisoners had to be housed in the Claiborne jail 35 miles away.[140]

An Indian village stood across the creek from Hampton Ridge, and for a while there was no friction between the Indians and the settlers. Trouble came when a distant band of Indians made a cattle-stealing raid in the vicinity. The settlers were quick to place the blame on the local Indians, armed themselves, and destroyed the Indian village. The Indians retreated, never to return.[141]

Many of the Hampton Ridge settlers promptly moved to the site of the Indian village and started a town, which they named Sparta, on the east bank of the creek. Soon this new town gained in population and became Hampton Ridge's chief rival for the county seat, winning the coveted prize in 1820.[142] Sparta became the center of county activities, and Hampton Ridge began to decline in importance. It never appeared on the state maps, dying in the early days of the state's history.

HANBYVILLE (Hanby's Mill, Hanby). This small village was on Turkey Creek, 1½ miles west of Pinson, in Jefferson County, but near the Blount County line. David Hanby first came into the Alabama Territory during the Creek War of 1813–14 as a blacksmith serving in the militia under General Andrew Jackson. As soon as the war ended, he returned to his home in Tennessee, returning later to Alabama where he settled as early as 1819,[143] although he did not enter his land legally until November 15, 1821.[144] Hanby built his home on Turkey Creek, near Hagood's Crossroads (now Pinson). In 1827 he and his sons erected a mill there expressly for grinding wheat. In 1840, he purchased nearby lands and began a career in coal mining.[145]

Michael Tuomey, the first state geologist of Alabama, in an early report stated that the seam of coal in this area was 20 inches thick and was "separated from the section above by a stratum of sandstone 15 feet in thickness. . . . Mr. Hanby is the proprietor, and is prospecting the work with as much energy as the force he can command will allow, where he has to begin with inexperienced hands."[146]

The "fat, jolly farmer," as Hanby was described by Mary Gordon Duffee,[147] employed a large force of men to work his mines. Not only were shafts used, but the men mined along the ridges of the hills and often were able to shovel the coal into flat-bottomed boats moored directly below them. During the winter months, these boats floated down the creek into the Black Warrior River, and from there into the Tombigbee to Mobile.[148]

In 1865, Wilson's Raiders came into the county and caused

many of the mining families to seek refuge in the wilderness of the hill country. One day as the elderly Hanby chatted with a group of Confederate soldiers, the Raiders made a surprise attack, in which the coal operator was shot and killed.[149]

HOLLOW SQUARE. The site of this once small village is located 1¾ miles northwest of Sawyerville, on Highway 14, in Hale County. The exact date of the founding of this village is not known. It first appeared on the state map in 1853. Early newspapers showed that a post office existed there in 1848.[150] County records indicate that John Q. A. Cleveland bought the mercantile establishment there from S. M. Cole in January, 1850.[151] In 1855, Isaac Snedecor described the village as "a minor one with a post office."[152] It was last seen on the state map in 1878.

HONEY CUT. This stage stop was approximately 17 miles southeast of the old town of Blakeley, in central Baldwin County. Tradition states that this area was first settled before 1800. It is known that the Hall family came there in 1808 from Pensacola.[153] Honey Cut was on the road from Blakeley to Pensacola, and a stagecoach stop and relay station were situated there.[154] It first appeared on the state map in 1853, and was last listed in 1878. Nothing is left today except for a small cemetery, the foundations of several buildings, the remains of a gristmill dam, and a well.

HOUSTON. Although one general store still remains in operation in this former county seat of Winston County, the town has virtually become a ghost town. It is situated just off U.S. Highway 278, between the towns of Double Springs and Addison. Winston County was created by the Alabama Legislature on February 12, 1850, from lands formerly held by Walker County. Houston became the county seat, a position that it retained until December, 1882, when Double Springs gained the county offices.[155]

Houston was the scene of wild excitement on Christmas Eve, 1860, when voters throughout the state went to the polls to vote for delegates to attend the Secession Convention in Montgomery.

From all over Winston County representatives gathered in Looney's Tavern, where the principal speaker was Charles C. Sheats, who had just been elected as the county's delegate. Elected as a cooperationist, Sheats vowed that if Alabama chose the road to secession from the Union, then Winston County would secede from the state of Alabama.[156]

On January 11, 1861, at the Alabama Secession Convention, 61 representatives voted for immediate secession, while Sheats and 38 others opposed the move. The Winston County delegate then refused to sign the Ordinance of Secession, returned home, refused to serve in the Confederate Army, and was forced to hide out in the hills.[157] Winston County was struck by bushwhacking throughout the war, so a crude form of civil war developed in the area. Sheats came out of hiding and began to recruit men for the 1st Alabama Union Cavalry, and was arrested and imprisoned for the remainder of the war by the state authorities.

After the war revenge slayings were common in the area. In the spring of 1867, Judge W. B. Wood ordered the erection of a jail in Houston, and a one-cell log structure was built, which stands in ruin there today.[158]

INDEPENDENCE. This dying little town is on Alabama Highway 19, approximately 14 miles west of Prattville, in Autauga County. The founding date of this farming village is not known. One of the earliest settlers in the area was Robert Motley, Sr., who cut timber and operated a mill 3 miles east of Independence. The town was first listed on the state map in 1830. With the decline of "King Cotton," Independence too declined. Nature struck the town a crushing blow in the spring of 1963. A tornado destroyed the local church, an institution that had seemed to hold the little town together. Today with the church gone and the school closed, little is left in the town except a small grocery store.[159]

IRONATON (Clifton). The site of this once populous town and mining center is on the western slope of the Talladega Mountains, 8 miles east of the city of Talladega and 10 miles south of Jenifer, in Talladega County. Long before the town of Ironaton existed, the site was owned by Rev. John Seay. In 1871, Sam and Stephen Noble purchased the property from the minister and started a mining town, which they called Clifton. A narrow gauge railroad was built to the town by the Nobles connecting it with their Clifton Iron Works.[160] The town consisted of two main streets and 4 miles of side streets. Blast furnaces, a company commissary, a city hall, a volunteer fire department, two hotels, and company cottages lined the streets.[161]

The town was incorporated on February 17, 1885, under the name of Ironaton. The population was 562 by the year 1890, 735 in 1900, and 982 in 1910. Around the year 1915, the town had its own electric light plant, a jail, a waterworks, two blast furnaces, a machine shop, a wood-working shop, and a sawmill. It was on the Atlanta, Birmingham and Atlantic Railroad. However, the town had reached the peak of its boom, for soon the mining interests failed, the inhabitants moved to other industrial areas, and Ironaton became a ghost town.[162]

JAMESTOWN (Warsaw). A former river landing, Jamestown was situated on the west bank of the Tombigbee River, 7½ miles north of Gainesville, and 4 miles east of Panola, in northwestern Sumter County. The area was first settled by the Little family and others from North Carolina in 1833–34. Members of the Little family operated large cotton plantations in the vicinity.[163] The landing first appeared on the state map in 1838 as Jamestown. The name Warsaw was first used in 1853, and is still what the people call the community. The town lost its importance with the decline of the steamboat trade and disappeared.[164]

JENIFER. The remains of this once busy iron manufacturing town are about 1 mile north of Munford and 12 miles northeast of Talladega, in Talladega County. During the winter of 1863, while the Civil War was raging throughout the Southland, James A. Curry and Samuel Clabaugh established an iron furnace, called the "Salt Creek Iron Works," on lands owned by Curry.[165] Croxton's Raiders destroyed the ironworks in April, 1865.[166] Three years after the war, the property was acquired by Horace

Ware, the owner of the Shelby Iron Works, who with the help of Stephen S. Glidden, rebuilt the ironworks and renamed them the "Alabama Furnace." A town was incorporated there on May 17, 1873.[167]

In 1881, Samuel Noble and A. L. Tyler, owners of the Clifton Iron Works at Ironaton, acquired the Alabama Furnace and changed the name of the town to Jenifer, in honor of Noble's mother, Mrs. Jenifer Ward Noble. Upon Noble's death in 1888 the works were sold to out-of-state owners.[168] The town was again incorporated on February 28, 1888, and at the time had a population of 500. By 1890 the population had decreased to 323, in 1900 to 331, and in 1910 to only 104.[169] Birmingham, in Jefferson County, had captured the iron trade and Jenifer died.

JONESBORO (Jonesborough). The site of this early Jefferson County settlement is today a portion of the grounds of the United States Cast Iron Pipe Company in the city of Bessemer. The valley of Jefferson County was named in honor of "Devil" John Jones, who came to the region in 1815 with his brother-in-law, Caleb Friley, and settled on the site that later became Jonesboro, also named in his honor.[170] They were joined by other pioneers, and although few Indians had been seen, these rugged settlers erected a crude stockade, which they called Fort Jonesborough.

John Thomas entered a land claim on July 31, 1821, and erected a mill and a cotton gin in the settlement.[171] Samuel A. Tarrant, the leading merchant of Jonesboro, established a hotel, which was said to be "a most agreeable and comfortable stopping place."[172] William Rose Sadler built the first grist and saw mill. His name appeared in the public records on September 10, 1819, when he entered land in the community.[173]

Volunteers from the community served in the Creek War of 1836, the Mexican War, and the Civil War.[174] After the Civil War, in 1866, Professor Isaac Wellington McAdory, late a lieutenant in the 28th Alabama Regiment, C.S.A., founded the Pleasant Hill Academy, an institution that he operated until 1888. It stood on the site of a school that had been built in 1828.[175] In the summer of 1886, Jonesboro was selected as a site for the erection of two iron furnaces. The following year the Bessemer Land Improvement Company was formed, which resulted in the founding of the "Marvel City," Bessemer, which absorbed tiny Jonesboro.[176]

KINGSTON. A former county seat of Autauga County, Kingston was situated approximately 8 miles northeast of the town of Independence, on or near U.S. Highway 82. Settlers migrated into Autauga County soon after the termination of the Creek War of 1813–14. The county was created on November 30, 1818, and the pioneer town of Washington became the first county seat (see Washington). Because Washington was in the southern part of the county, people were dissatisfied with it as county seat. On December 2, 1830, the Alabama Legislature appointed commissioners to select a more central site for the seat of justice. Kingston was chosen because of its location, but many people referred to it as the "Great Sahara."[177]

One of Kingston's most influential citizens was a former Englishman, Captain William N. Thompson, who had come to the county in 1820 and erected a saw and grist mill on Swift Creek, where the town of Autaugaville now stands. When Kingston became the county seat, Thompson moved into the town and built a tavern, a public house, and a store. He died in the town in 1851.[178] On December 12, 1868, the county seat was removed to Prattville,[179] and Kingston soon became a ghost town.

LAGRANGE. This college town was 4 miles southwest of Leighton, and approximately 9 miles southeast of Tuscumbia, in Franklin County. Probably it originated around the year 1820, and was first known as a summer resort area for the wealthy Tennessee Valley planters. It was named in honor of the Frenchman who invented the metric system. At one time LaGrange contained over 400 people.[180]

Soon after General Lafayette's visit to Alabama in 1825 a high school was established at LaGrange, which was named the Lafayette Academy. Under the presidency of Rev. Daniel P. Bestor, the school prospered, and was housed in a large two-storied brick building. Boys who graduated from the school were prepared for entrance into the town's college.[181]

LaGrange College, founded by the Methodist Church, opened its doors on January 11, 1830, and served the community for twenty-eight years. In 1858, the college was removed to Florence, where it became Florence Wesleyan, and the old buildings and grounds then became the LaGrange College and Military Academy, which reached its peak of enrollment in 1861 with 171 students.[182]

The town of LaGrange extended over an area of more than a mile and was the site of many fine homes. The former Baptist church was sold to the Methodists in 1851 and became the center of the college community. Dry goods stores, grocery stores, a blacksmith shop, a tannery, a woodworking shop, a post office, a tailoring shop, and the Masonic Hall graced the city streets.[183]

Early in the Civil War the 35th Alabama Regiment was organized in the town. On April 28, 1863, Union Colonel Florence N. Cornyn and members of the 10th Missouri Cavalry destroyed the military college and also burned hundreds of homes and businesses, including the Lafayette Academy. The town and schools were never rebuilt.[184]

LARKIN'S FORK. Situated in a fork of Paint Rock Creek, this small town was approximately 12 miles southeast of New Market, and 6 miles north of Princeton, in Jackson County. This town should not be confused with Larkinsville, which is also in the county. Larkin's Fork was first listed on the state map in 1842, located at a crossroads, one route going from Tennessee to Trenton, and another from New Market to Bellefonte.[185] Never very large, it disappeared from the map in the early years of the twentieth century.

LEXINGTON. This short-lived town was on the south bank of Hatchemadega Creek, approximately 25 miles north of Wetumpka, in Coosa County. On November 28, 1833, the Alabama Legislature appointed four commissioners to select a seat of justice for the new county of Coosa. They made their choice of 160 acres of land, which was divided into lots and sold at public auction. Thus Lexington came into existence, situated within 8 miles of the center of the county.[186]

County records indicate that the first meeting of the commissioners' court was held in the town in May, 1834. During the following term of the court, held in August, 1834, the construction of roads was ordered.[187] Within the same year, the county seat was abandoned in favor of the town of Rockford.[188] It is not known if any public buildings were ever erected in Lexington. It last appeared on the state map in 1842, but soon afterwards became merely a portion of the plantation of Albert Crumpler.

LITTLE WARRIOR. The site of this small village was 10 miles southwest of Oneonta and 11 miles south of Blountsville, approximately 2 miles east of the confluence of the Locust Fork and the Little Black Warrior River, in Blount County. A post office was established in the village on January 29, 1852, with Henson D. Harbin serving as postmaster until the office was closed on January 7, 1867. On August 31, 1869, the post office was again established, but was discontinued on February 8, 1875. On March 8, 1875, it was revived for the third time, but was finally closed forever on August 14, 1905.[189]

LOUINA. Situated in southwestern Randolph County, this small town was on the east bank of the Tallapoosa River, near Wadley. The town was named in honor of an Indian woman who had established a trading post on the site. It was one of three trading points in the early days of the county's history, a history which began on December 18, 1832, when the Alabama Legislature created Randolph County. The settlers could cross the river at this town on Hunter's ferry. Louina, the Indian, sold her establishment in 1836 when the Creeks moved to the West.[190] The exact date of the town's demise is not known, but it was still listed on maps in the early 1900s.

MCINTOSH BLUFF. Alabama's first county seat was on a bluff on the west bank of the Tombigbee River, 18 miles north of the 31st parallel and 40 miles north of Mobile, near McIntosh, in Washington County. In 1775, during the British period of Alabama history, Captain John McIntosh, of the British Army, received a grant of 500 acres including the bluff that bears his name, the former home site of the Tahome Indians, on which he established his home and plantation. During the American Revolution, he refused to stand behind the colonists, and therefore was forced to abandon his property when the war ended.[191] In 1776, Thomas Bassett received 750 acres including the bluff. He also held a grant of 1,050 acres near the mouth of the creek that still bears his name. He was killed in 1781 by Indians while returning from a trip to Pensacola.[192] Washington County was created on June 4, 1800, within the Mississippi Territory, and McIntosh Bluff was selected as the first county seat. In September, 1802, the county court convened for the first time with Judge Seth Lewis presiding. During the following year Lorenzo Dow visited the town and preached the first sermon there.[193] In 1805, the county seat was changed to nearby Wakefield (see Wakefield). However, when Baldwin County was created on December 21, 1809 from land taken from Washington County, Wakefield fell on the Baldwin County side of the line, so the seat was returned to McIntosh Bluff.[194] McIntosh Bluff retained the county seat until December, 1820, when the boundary was again altered and the town became a part of Mobile County. The court of Mobile ordered that the former courthouse and jail be sold, and the money received was divided between Mobile and Baldwin counties.[195] In 1828, the boundary was once again changed and the old town was once again a part of Washington County, but by this time it had almost disappeared.[196]

MARDISVILLE (Jumper's Spring). The remains of this early town are on U.S. Highway 231, approximately halfway between the town of Winterboro and the city of Talladega, in Talladega County. By the cession of Creek Indian lands in 1832, nine new counties were created in Alabama. Talladega County was one of the nine. A crude log cabin was immediately erected at Jumper's Spring to house the office of the Coosa Land District, where Leonard Tarrant, a minister of the Gospel, was the certifying agent.[197] Force-Hatchie-Fixico, the chieftain of the Talladega Indians, who was commonly known to the whites as "Jumper," sold his lands in the vicinity before he died. The whites who were living in the community of Jumper's Spring, whether out of a feeling of guilt or love, acquired a coffin for the old Indian and the ladies made him a long white shroud. The funeral was then conducted, after which the body was buried in a sitting position, according to tribal custom, in the corner of the chieftain's cabin. Later that night, tradition states that drunken Indians exhumed the body and one of them rode away into the darkness wearing the shroud.[198]

Several months after the creation of the land office at Jumper's Spring, the citizens renamed the rapidly growing community Mardisville, in honor of Samuel W. Mardis, a congressman who had been instrumental in obtaining the treaty with the Indians.[199]

Homes and businesses were established in the town. John Hardie erected a general store and lived 1½ miles from town on his 1,700-acre plantation, Thornhill. Across from Hardie's store stood a large two-story tavern, behind which stood the harness and repair shop of David Waugh. A Presbyterian church and a Methodist church served the religious needs of the inhabitants. There were also a dry goods store, a bakery, a woodworking shop, and academies for both males and females.[200]

The decline of Mardisville began in the mid 1830s, because of business competition from nearby Talladega. Death was slow. By the turn of the century the tavern, most of the stores, the churches, and the academies had been abandoned.

MELTON'S BLUFF (Marathon). This early county seat was at the head of the Elk River shoals, on the south bank of the Tennessee River, in Lawrence County. Today the site lies below the waters of the Tennessee River, 2 miles above Lock A. Lawrence County was created by the Alabama Legislature on February 4, 1818, and Melton's Bluff was selected as the seat of the county government. At that time it was the largest town in the county and the first to be founded. The town was named in honor of John Melton, an Irishman who had come into the area many years before because of his displeasure with his fellow man. There he married a Cherokee woman and raised a family. This unfriendly man accumulated a fortune by robbing pioneers on the flatboats traveling on the river below the bluff. With this money he purchased many slaves and established a tavern. When he died around the year 1815, his plantation was bought by Andrew Jackson, who worked it with 60 slaves.[201]

Later Jackson and his associate John Coffee had the bluff surveyed and divided into 658 lots for a town, hoping to attract settlers to compete with the nearby town of Bainbridge (see Bainbridge). Anne Newport Royall, a visitor in 1818, described the beauty of the site.[202] After 1819, the town was listed on state maps as Marathon. In 1820 the county seat was removed to Moulton, an act which killed Marathon.[203] It was last listed on a state map in 1850.

MEMPHIS. On the west bank of the Tombigbee River, this river landing was approximately 8 miles west of Aliceville, in southwestern Pickens County. The town was founded in 1841 by James Williamson Wallis, whose foresight had led him to recognize the value of the site, which was in a large bend of the river. His wife was so proud of being the cofounder of the town that she had the words "Mother of Memphis" carved on her tombstone.[204]

Soon after Wallis had founded the town there were more than fifty families living in comfortable homes along Cotton Street, the principal thoroughfare, and along other streets of the town. A fine hotel was erected and several warehouses, a church, a school, a post office, 2 saloons, and more than 8 general stores.[205] Memphis began to decline when the railroads captured much of the former trade of the steamboats. After the Civil War, the Mobile and Ohio Railroad bypassed the town, running through nearby Aliceville instead. Therefore, by March 14, 1892, the date on which James Wallis died, the town had already become a ghost town.[206]

MIDDLETON. This small town was situated between Pigeon Creek and Patsaliga Creek, approximately 16 miles south of Greenville, in Butler County. First appearing on the state map in 1838, this town was on the road between Greenville and Montezuma, the county seat of Covington County (see Montezuma).[207] It disappeared from the map after the Civil War period.

MONTEZUMA. An early county seat of Covington County, Montezuma was situated on the east bank of the Conecuh River, 4 miles east of its confluence with Patsaliga Creek. Covington County was created by the Alabama Legislature on December 18, 1821. On December 12, 1822, five commissioners were appointed to select the site for the county seat, and Montezuma was their choice. Little is known about the town. In 1847, it was destroyed by an overflow of the Conecuh River, and the county offices were moved to New Site (now Andalusia), which was 4 miles to the south.[208]

NAVY COVE. This small community was on the north side of Mobile Point which faces the Bay, 3 miles east of Fort Morgan, in Baldwin County. This antebellum village was founded by the families of oyster fishermen and ship pilots. It never contained any hotels or boarding houses, yet visitors did come to the community to purchase oysters and to enjoy the sun and sand.

In the summer of 1906, there were 14 homes and around 40 inhabitants living at Navy Cove. On September 5, of that year, a violent hurricane struck savagely along the coast, and at the conclusion of the storm hardly anything remained of the community. Six lives were lost, and even the land was changed by the vicious waves. Sand knolls disappeared and many home sites lay under the waters of the Bay.

Five members of the family of Captain Denny Ladnier were killed, including his wife and four sons. The Captain and his daughters survived by floating in the branches of a large tree. The site of their home now lies 10 feet beneath the waters of the Bay.

Three dozen inhabitants were saved when they retreated to four large oak trees situated on a knoll. They tied a rope securely around the trees and desperately clung to it until the winds died down. After the storm had subsided, most of the inhabitants of Navy Cove moved away to other communities.[209]

NEW BOSTON. Little is known about this small town, which was situated 6 miles east of Russellville, in Franklin County. It was first listed on the state map in 1838 on the road between Russellville and Moulton and was last listed in 1856.[210]

NEW BOSTON. This small village was approximately 5 miles north of Dayton and 6 miles southeast of Old Spring Hill, in Marengo County. Very little information exists pertaining to the history of the village. It first appeared on the state map in 1838,[211] and was last listed on a state map in 1850. W. C. Tharin did not mention it in his *A Directory of Marengo County for 1860–61*.

NEW LONDON. This small town was situated approximately 6 miles north of the dead town of Thornhill, and about 22 miles southwest of Moulton, in Winston County. Little is known about the town, which first appeared on a state map in 1838, situated at a junction in the road from Moulton to Pikeville and the road between New London to Tuscaloosa.[212] It was last listed on a map in 1856.

NEW RIVER. A small community situated in what is today the Hubbertville community, New River was approximately 15 miles northeast of Fayette, in Fayette County. Very little is known about this antebellum community. A post office was established there on August 11, 1853, with Hugh W. McCaleb serving as postmaster. The office was closed before the end of the Civil War, but reestablished on August 19, 1869, and continued in operation until 1911.[213]

NEWTOWN. This early town has been completely absorbed by Tuscaloosa. At one time the dividing line between the two adjoining towns was 32nd Avenue. The U.S. Congress passed an act on March 3, 1819, granting 36 square miles of land in Alabama to the Connecticut Deaf and Dumb Asylum. William H. Ely, as agent of the Asylum, came to the state in 1820 to select the property, which would be sold to bring money to the noteworthy institution. He first selected lands in Jefferson County (see Elyton), and then chose 4½ sections west and south of the then small village of Tuscaloosa. By so doing he stopped or blocked the boundaries of the existing town from growing, causing much resentment in the "Druid City."[214]

To remedy this situation, on January 17, 1821, a group of twelve men purchased the Asylum's lands, and incorporated it into a town first known as "The Lower Part of the Town of Tuscaloosa," and which was soon after referred to as "Newtown." The site was surveyed and people rushed in to purchase lots.[215]

Soon afterwards the voters of Tuscaloosa County chose to build the courthouse there. William Rufus Smith stated that it was erected "on a spot about three hundred yards southwest of the site on which the State Capitol was afterwards built."[216] He also wrote that "the village of New Town began to assume beautiful proportions, having one business street compactly built with commodious storehouses, many of them of brick, of handsome finish and large dimensions, while in the center of this street was a snug little brickpillared market house. There were, at one time, ten or twelve active and thriving business establishments in New Town; a row of law offices and doctor's shops, and an extensive hotel."[217]

On the morning of March 4, 1842, a tornado struck the town, destroying the courthouse, the hotel, and many homes, killing one young girl. The town was later rebuilt, but never again did it reach the importance of former years. The courthouse was erected in Tuscaloosa, and gradually the old town became a part of the "Druid City."[218]

NEW YORK (York Bluff). This early town was across the Tennessee River from the mouth of Cypress Creek, within the boundaries of the city of Sheffield, in Colbert County. The site of an early French trading post, this land was acquired by Andrew Jackson and John Coffee just after the Creek Indian War of 1813–14, and was surveyed for a town. It only lasted for a short time and soon was doomed when its neighbor, Ococoposa (Tuscumbia) was incorporated as a town on December 20, 1820.[219]

NOTTINGHAM. The "town which never was" was on Talladega Creek, 1 mile northeast of the village of Alpine and 5 miles southeast of Talladega, in Talladega County. During the steelmaking boom of the 1880s, C. D. Morrison, a New Yorker, purchased a plantation near Alpine on which he proposed to erect a large city—Nottingham. In 1886, the Nottingham Iron and Land Company was formed, and by 1889 plans were made to establish two large furnaces, each with a capacity of 65 tons. The 540-acre town site was surveyed and divided into 1,830 lots and sales proceeded.[220]

By 1890, the site had 15 duplexes, a restaurant, and storehouses. An announcement was then made that an electric plant and a waterworks were soon to be established. The Selma, Rome and Dalton Railroad finished a stationhouse 100 feet away from the spot where workmen were busy building the Nottingham Hotel, a sixty-room, two-story frame edifice.[221] The hotel opened on April 29, 1890, with a memorable dance, which was given to celebrate the festive occasion. For the next six months prospective buyers and businessmen resided at the establishment, coming from as far away as New York and Pennsylvania.[222]

In the spring of 1887, a contractor dug a large hole for the foundation of one of the furnaces, but then the enthusiasm for the enterprise began to disappear. The furnace project ceased, and the investors and businessmen rushed in panic to sell their properties in the town.[223] Soon the hotel closed its doors because of a lack of visitors, and in 1895 the building was sold for salvage for only $750.[224] The town that had been born in optimism died a quick death in its infancy.

OREGONIA. This small village was situated approximately 22 miles north of Tuscaloosa and 11 miles east of New Lexington, in Tuscaloosa County. Oregonia first appeared on a state map in 1853, on the road between Tuscaloosa and Decatur.[225] Very little information exists pertaining to its history. A Baptist Church was founded there in 1865.[226] It remained on the map until the early years of the twentieth century.

PIKEVILLE. The site of this early town is on the southeastern bank of the Buttahatchee River near its north fork. It may be reached by traveling 7 miles north of Guin on U.S. Highway 278, in Marion County. Marion County, created by the territorial legislature on December 13, 1818, was settled by pioneers coming from the Carolinas and Tennessee. In 1819, the home of Henry Grier was chosen as a temporary county seat, and this home became the foundation of the town of Pikeville. On the early maps it was listed simply as "C.H." (Courthouse).[227]

The town retained the coveted county seat until 1882, when Captain Albert J. Hamilton donated 40 acres in the town of Toll Gate to the county. Toll Gate became the county seat and was renamed Hamilton. Pikeville gradually declined into a ghost town.[228]

PIPER. A coal-mining town, Piper was 5 miles east of West Blocton and 11 miles north of Centreville, on the east bank of the Cahaba River, in Bibb County. Located in the heart of the Cahaba Coal Field, Piper was developed as the site of a mine, which furnished coal to the iron industry of Birmingham via the Louisville and Nashville Railroad.[229] Only two families live today in the community that once furnished an income to 2,000 people and supported a school and several stores.

The decline of the coal industry reduced the population to 75 families soon after World War II. A cave-in occurred around 1950, so the mine was closed. The inhabitants then moved to nearby West Blocton or to Birmingham, and the school ceased operations in 1954. The school, depot, stores, and most of the houses have been razed, and only a pond marks the site.[230]

PORTERSVILLE. This coastal town was on approximately the same site as the present-day town of Coden, 2 miles south of Bayou La Batre, in southern Mobile County. In the days of the French colony in Alabama, the coastal area now known as Bayou Coden was then known as "Coq d'Inde" (turkey).[231] Later, in Spanish times, the first recorded inhabitant was listed in the records as Barthelemy Grelot, who only lived there a short time. Eighteen months later (1786), Joseph Bousage lived there with his family.[232]

Portersville first appeared on a state map in 1838; the descendants of the French were engaged in the seafood business. During this period, travelers moving between the cities of Mobile and New Orleans would take the stage from Mobile to Portersville and a boat from there to Lake Pontchartrain, and then travel to New Orleans by rail.[233]

Portersville did not appear on the state map after 1870, and Coden was listed in the same area after the turn of the century.

PRAIRIE BLUFF (Prairie Blue). A river landing on a high bluff on the north bank of the Alabama River in the section of the river known as Canton Bend, Prairie Bluff was near the present-day Miller's Ferry Bridge, in Wilcox County. It was listed on the Lucas map in 1819 and on the state map in 1822 as "Prairie Blue," but on all subsequent maps as "Prairie Bluff." A road linked the bluff with the town of Cahaba to the northeast and to St. Stephens to the southwest.

A large cotton slide was erected from the top of the bluff to the wharf below, much like the one at Claiborne. An engraving showing the work of loading cotton at night displayed an interesting picture of blacks laboring under the lights from many torches.[234]

Excitement prevailed at the landing on October 28, 1841, when the steamboat *Jewess* struck a snag and sank in the area. The same fate had befallen a smaller steamer, the *Pittsburg*, there in May, 1828.[235] The landing reached its peak of importance in 1861, but after the Civil War the railroads captured the once profitable river trade and the town died.

RAWLINGSVILLE. This small town was about 3 miles north of Fort Payne, and approximately 12 miles southwest of Valley Head, in De Kalb County. This small road junction town was first listed on a state map in 1846, on roads running eastward and northeastward into Georgia. It was last listed on the map in 1878, and declined as its neighbor, Fort Payne, began to thrive.

RED BLUFF (Centreport, Elm Bluff). Situated on the east bank of the Alabama River, this early landing was approximately 5 miles north of the landing at Portland, and 14 miles down the river from the old state capital at Cahaba, in Dallas County. H. S. Tanner's map of Alabama, published in 1830, showed Red Bluff on a road that led 9 miles northward to the ferry at Cahaba, and southward where it intersected the Montgomery to Blakeley road. Another road, with Red Bluff at its upper end, moved southeastward to Fort Dale, where it also intersected the Montgomery to Blakeley road. On the 1838 map, the landing was listed as "Centreport."

The most prominent citizen living in the area was John J. Crocheron, who came to Dallas County from New York state, and built a beautiful mansion, Elm Bluff, in 1840.[236] After the Civil War years, the landing was listed on the maps as Elm Bluff. It disappeared from the maps after 1878, as the railroads captured the river trade.

REHOBOTH. The site of this small village is on the farm of Laird Love and family, near Chilatchee Creek, just north of the Canton Bend of the Alabama River, approximately 4 miles southeast of Gastonburg, in Wilcox County. Very little is known about the history of this village, which once contained stores, a hotel, the Rehoboth Male Academy (a private boarding school), and a number of homes. The cemetery of the church (for which the village was named) contains many graves; the oldest burial dates from the 1840s. The private cemetery of the Young family, surrounded by an iron fence, stands at the side of the village.[237]

The village was not listed on the state maps until the early 1860s. It prospered during the latter half of the nineteenth century and died approximately fifty years ago. The antebellum home of the late John Laird, educator, is still occupied by his sisters; the family originally had come from South Carolina just after the Civil War. The ruins of two other large antebellum homes are still standing, but all of the other buildings of the village, including the church, are gone.[238]

RENFROE. This industrial town was 5 miles west of the city of Talladega, on the west side of the Sleeping Giant's Mountain, in Talladega County. In 1884, the D. W. Rogers and Company established a large saw and planing mill on this site around which grew the community of Renfroe, containing the homes of the lumber workers. The town was incorporated by the state legislature on February 22, 1887, and had a population of 1,000. The Atlanta, Birmingham, and Coast Railroad went through the town, hauling the lumber products to market. A beautiful little lake was developed with artistic bridges for the enjoyment of the citizens.[239]

Unfortunately, the prosperity of Renfroe was shortlived. Associates of the D. W. Rogers and Company resigned and established another lumbering concern near Stemley in 1889, and after a few years the Rogers mill at Renfroe ceased operations. The lake was drained, and an act was approved to repeal the incorporation of the town on December 8, 1900. At that time the population had fallen to only 180 persons, and a decade later there were only 85 in the town. The final death blow came in 1956 when the post office was closed.[240]

RICHMOND (Wiggin's Springs). A former county seat, this site was approximately 10 miles east of Newton, in Dale County. The Alabama Legislature created Henry County on December 13, 1819. At that time the county consisted of a very large area of land, including much of present-day Henry, Dale, Coffee, and Geneva counties, and parts of Pike, Crenshaw, and Barbour counties. The town of Richmond, formerly known as Wiggin's Springs, was an early seat of the county.[241]

On December 22, 1824, Dale County was created from parts of Henry, Covington, Barbour, and Pike counties. Richmond fell within the boundaries of this new county, and an act of December 20, 1827, stated that the circuit court of Dale would be located in the old Richmond courthouse.[242] On January 26, 1829, the circuit court was moved away from Richmond to the home of Creede Collins, so the town lost its former importance. The final blow came on December 8, 1830, when the county judge and commissioners of roads and revenue put the old courthouse and jail up for sale to be razed.[243]

ROCKY HILL. The site of this early village is approximately 10 miles north of the eastern end of the Cochrane Bridge, in Baldwin County. Very little is known about Rocky Hill. It was first listed on a state map in 1830, on the road between Blakeley and Montgomery. It was last listed on the map in 1850.

ST. STEPHENS. The historic site is 9 miles northwest of Leroy, on the west bank of the Tombigbee River, in Washington County. French inhabitants of old Mobile knew the bluff, which the Indians called Hobucakintopa. However, because the site lay 60 miles north of the port city, they never established a post there. On January 14, 1772, during the British occupation of Alabama, an explorer, Bernard Romans, visited the bluff and recorded: "Stout sloops and schooners may come up to this rapid; therefore, I judge some considerable settlement will take place."[244]

Early in 1789, the Governor of Spanish Mobile, Juan Vincente Folch, ordered Lieutenant José Deville Degoutin to erect a fort on Hobucakintopa Bluff (see Fort St. Stephens in Part II). After finding the fort in a deplorable condition in 1795, Lieutenant Antonio Palao rebuilt it with cypress logs and placed an infantry garrison there. The garrison halted Indian raids in the vicinity and served as a post for trade with the Choctaws.[245]

American settlers, many evading the law, flocked into the area. A census of the area taken in 1796 showed that there were 190 white settlers and 97 Negro slaves there, of which 89 percent had come from the United States.[246]

By the terms of the Treaty of San Lorenzo, the Americans took charge of the fort on February 5, 1799.[247] In 1803, Joseph Chambers was appointed the agent of the Choctaw Trading House, a government trading post at St. Stephens.[248] In March, 1805, George Strother Gaines took charge of the agency and found that the old Spanish blockhouse was being used as the company's store. He made his home in the former home of the Spanish commandant. A land office was housed in the former "warhouse."[249] In 1811, Gaines constructed a brick house to serve as a warehouse, probably the first brick building erected by Americans in Alabama.[250]

On April 6, 1804, President Thomas Jefferson appointed Ephraim Kirby of Connecticut, as the first superior court judge of the Mississippi Territory. Judge Kirby was not pleased with the inhabitants of this area and informed the President that "this section of the United States has long afforded an asylum to those who prefer voluntary exile to punishments ordained by law for heinous offences. The present inhabitants (with few exceptions) are illiterate, wild and savage, of depraved morals, unworthy of public confidence or private esteem; litigious, disunited, and knowing each other, universally distrustful of each other. . . . "[251] Lorenzo Dow, the pioneer minister, shared Kirby's views, but added that "since it [St. Stephens] fell to us, it seems to be a hopeful way, but there is still room for great amendment." Two years later, in 1805, he again visited, found many improvements, and predicted that the area would be "a place of fame in time."[252]

An act was approved by the Mississippi Territorial Legislature in 1807 to incorporate a town at St. Stephens, a survey was made, and lots were promptly sold. During the Creek War of 1813–14, refugees from the surrounding area flocked to the town for safety, and after the war the town prospered. In 1816, there were 40 houses where only a year before there were but 9. The St. Stephens Academy was chartered, being the first school in Washington County.[253]

The Alabama Territory was created on March 3, 1817, with St. Stephens as its capital. William Wyatt Bibb, the first and only territorial governor, directed the newly formed government, which met in two rooms of the Douglas Hotel. Business in the town thrived during this period.

St. Stephens was the site of the Tombecbe Bank, the first bank to be chartered in the state. Its first president was Israel Pickens, who would later become the third governor of Alabama. According to an account written by Miss Mary Welsh the bank "was suddenly terminated by a robbery, which caused a wild and widespread tumult at the time. But the guilty party was never discovered, and a mystery still shrouds the robbery . . . "[254]

When Alabama became a state in 1819, Cahaba was selected to serve as the first capital, an act causing business to decline at St. Stephens. By 1833, it had become but a small village at an important road junction. Soon after this time an epidemic of yellow fever swept through the area. By the time of the Civil War the town had all but disappeared. On May 6, 1899, the "Spanish Evacuation Centennial" was held in what had been St. Stephens, which at the time was only a wilderness with a few overgrown ruins.[255]

SHELBY SPRINGS. Once a popular watering place, this site is today a large cattle ranch, lying just off Highway 25 between Calera and Columbiana, in Shelby County. Early settlers in this area marveled at the medicinal properties of these springs. They were first developed into a resort in 1839. In 1855, the popularity of the resort became greater than ever because the Tennessee and Alabama River Railroad was linked with the site. A two-story hotel was erected with a walkway leading to the railroad station.

Many cabins dotted the 2,700-acre landscape.[256]

During the Civil War, in 1862, the resort became a training ground for Confederate troops and was known as Camp Winn. Later in the war, the hotel and cabins were converted into a hospital known as the Shelby Springs Hospital, a 350-bed facility.[257]

In 1869, the area once again became a resort. The old hotel was destroyed by fire in 1881, but a new one was built and placed into operation in 1887. The new facility was destroyed by fire in 1896. A building for dining and dancing was soon erected, and cottages provided sleeping accommodations for the guests.[258] A new hotel was built in 1905, but it too was destroyed by fire in 1910. The management continued to lease cottages until 1915, when the resort was closed forever.[259]

SHELBYVILLE. This early county seat of Shelby County was approximately 12 miles northeast of Montevallo. Shelby County was created on February 7, 1817, two years before Alabama became a state, and Shelbyville served as the first county seat. Named in honor of Governor Isaac Shelby of Kentucky, the town was situated on a road from Selma to Blountsville.[260]

County records indicate that on January 4, 1820, the sum of 53 dollars was paid to Thomas Amis Rogers for the erection of a courthouse, which was "twenty-four feet long, twenty feet wide, eight feet to the eaves; clap-board roof; lined and chinked—with benches—door with shutters . . . "[261] In 1821, commissioners were chosen to select a permanent county seat. Columbia (now Columbiana) became the seat in 1826. Shelbyville disappeared from the state map after the Civil War period.[262]

SOUTH PORT (South Florence). This early port was directly across the Tennessee River from Florence, and 2 miles northeast of Tuscumbia, in Colbert County. Pioneers were able to travel from the Muscle Shoals along the Military Road to the upper reaches of the Tombigbee River. A ferry was established in 1817 at the site of the present U.S. Highway 43 bridge, and soon the southern landing became a flourishing port, known as South Port.[263]

During the early 1820s, there were eight warehouses in the town. However, in a decade the port seemed to be dying when much of the population moved away to nearby Tuscumbia with the arrival of the Tuscumbia to Decatur Railroad. In 1841, prosperity was revived when the firm of Price and Simpson opened a general retail store in the town, which was then called South Florence. Warehouse sheds were erected to handle the cotton trade for that section of North Alabama. From 1841 until 1852, an annual average of 12,000 bales was shipped from the port city to New Orleans, and from 1852 until the Civil War an average of 16,000 bales was shipped. The warehouse sheds were destroyed during the war, and afterwards the landing at Tuscumbia took over this river trade.[264]

SPARTA. This early county seat was just to the east of Murder Creek, 10 miles southeast of Bellville, in Conecuh County. In 1818, Hampton Ridge became the first county seat of Conecuh County (see Hampton Ridge). During that same year, Malachi Warren built a cabin on the site of what would later become the town of Sparta, and he also established a small grocery store.[265] Pioneer families soon placed their homes in the vicinity of the store.

In 1819, a crude inn was constructed out of pine poles in the area, and this hostel became known as the Gauf House. Dr. Jonathan Shaw, a physician from the North moved into the inn and began practice in the little town.[266]

A bitter rivalry broke out between the Hampton Ridge settlers and the people living around Warren's store. An election was held in 1820 in which it was decided to move the county seat to Sparta, as Warren's community was then called. Thomas Watts, a lawyer who had been living there for a year, suggested the name "Sparta" in honor of his former home in Georgia.[267] The courthouse in Sparta was constructed of pine logs and measured 20 by 30 feet. Because there was no church in town, this crude building served a double purpose. Three years later a more appropriate church structure was erected.[268]

Sparta continued to thrive, and in 1856 the town boasted of having the first newspaper in the county. Also at this time much enthusiasm was created over the prospect of having a railroad established through the county, connecting Montgomery with Pensacola. At a public barbecue citizens subscribed $85,000 toward the prosperous enterprise and construction began almost immediately, although the road was not finished until 1861. In 1858, a telegraph line was completed between the town and Mobile.[269]

On March 21, 1865, Union raiders, under the command of Colonel A. B. Spurling, advanced into Conecuh County from Milton, Florida. On the 23rd, they struck at Pollard, at Evergreen, and reached Sparta at four o'clock in the afternoon. They burned the depot, the jail, and some railroad trestles, and destroyed the rolling stock found in the area.[270]

In 1866, the county seat was removed to Evergreen, after the courthouse at Sparta was destroyed by a fire.[271] The town declined in importance and eventually disappeared from the map.

SPRINGFIELD. This early Greene County town was 3 miles northeast of Eutaw. Settlers arrived in the northern section of Greene County in 1818. Springfield first appeared on state maps in 1830, at that time one of two towns within the present boundaries of Greene County. Large cotton plantations were established in the vicinity. The "sporting gentry" among the wealthy formed the Springfield Jockey Club. Austin Pollard, the secretary of the club, advertised races that were held in the town for 3 days in November, 1836.[272]

While the county seat was at Erie, Springfield was the most important town in northern Greene County, but it was soon surpassed in 1838 by Eutaw when it became the county seat and robbed nearby Springfield of its prosperity. By 1855, only 2 dry goods stores, a church, and 40 inhabitants remained in the old town, which ceased to exist entirely after the Civil War.[273]

STRINGER. This community was situated 4 miles southeast of Somerville, approximately 1 mile south of the crossing of Highways 36 and 37, in Morgan County. The Stringer family came to Morgan County from Kentucky around 1822. One member of the family, Edward Stringer, is recorded as having received lands in the Gandy's Cove area in 1831. Later, in 1852, he obtained the land that became the site of Stringer.[274]

This small town has changed locations on three different occasions. It absorbed the post office of what had been known as Fort Bluff in 1891. The last site of the town was on Six Mile Creek. The town died in 1909 when the post office was closed.[275]

SUNNYSIDE (Triana Ferry Landing). A former Tennessee River port, Sunnyside was on the south bank of the river 1 mile east of the mouth of Cataco Creek, in Morgan County. Little recorded history pertains to this shortlived port. A post office was there from 1888 to 1890 but was removed in May, 1890, to nearby Talucah.[276]

THORNHILL. This small town was approximately 21 miles north of Eldridge, near the Natural Bridge, in Winston County. The first post office in what later became Winston County opened there in 1836–37.[277] The town appeared on the state map in 1842, at the junction of a road from Moulton to Pikeville and another from Thornhill to Jasper. It was last listed on the map in 1878.

TRIANA. This river port was on the north bank of the Tennessee River approximately 8 miles southeast of Mooresville and 12 miles southwest of Huntsville, on the west bank of the mouth of Barren Branch, in Madison County. This port was founded at the southern terminus of the Indian Creek Canal. At the time of its founding, lots were selling for as high as $1,500 for a 60-foot lot. The town was incorporated on November 13, 1819 and was one of the first six voting precincts in the county.[278] Triana become less important as other river ports were founded but remained on the state map until early in the twentieth century. It lost most of its importance just before the Civil War when a railroad was established between Huntsville and the river port at Decatur.

UPPER PEACH TREE. Situated on the west bank of the Alabama River, just north of the mouth of Turkey Creek, this former river landing was approximately 12 miles west of Camden, in Wilcox County. George Morgan was the first settler in this area, arriving in 1816.[279] The town first appeared on the state map in

1838 but disappeared after the Civil War years. Its end was probably caused by the coming of the railroad, destroying the freight business on the rivers.

VALHERMOSO SPRINGS. This once famous resort town was situated on Highway 36 in northeastern Morgan County, approximately 20 miles northeast of Hartselle and 12 miles south of Huntsville. These mineral springs were probably discovered by Lancelot Chunn sometime just after 1810. They were referred to as Chunn Springs by the early pioneers. Between 1818 and 1823, a hotel was erected on the site, which was known as the White Sulphur Springs Hotel. In May, 1834, a post office was established, but it was closed in June, 1835.[280]

Jean Joseph Giers, a native of Germany, acquired the site in 1856 and renamed it Valhermoso Springs, meaning "Vale of Beauty." He purchased the 1,200 acres for only a dollar an acre and became postmaster when the post office was reestablished in 1857. Giers' Cedar Hotel was a three-story building surrounded by a number of cottages.[281] Ernst Giers, the son of the owner, acquired the property when his father died on December 16, 1880, and operated it until 1920. A tornado, followed by a fire, destroyed the building in 1950, and today the area is only a rural community.[282]

VERNON. This early Autauga County town was on a high bluff on the north bank of the Alabama River just east of the mouth of Swift Creek. Vernon was founded about 1819 by Seaborn Mims and his wife, who were natives of Georgia. Other settlers soon followed and the town was incorporated on December 8, 1821.[283]

Vernon Landing, a place where cotton could be shipped to Mobile, became the focal point of the surrounding countryside. A firm owned by John H. Southerland and Albert McNeel and another owned by Theodore Nunn and W. N. Thompson conducted most of the town's mercantile business.[284] Vernon was an active place of business until about 1848 when Autaugaville became prominent and took away most of the trade from the older town. In 1886, the Autauga County historian, Shadrack Mims, stated that all that remained of the town was a dilapidated warehouse.[285]

VIENNA. This Pickens County river port was on the northern bank of the Upper Tombigbee River, 2 miles north of the Sipsy Fork and 7 miles south of Aliceville. Vienna first appeared on the state map in 1830 at the point where Bear Creek emptied into the Tombigbee. In the early days of the county's history a ferry was in operation there. The town was for many years an important steamboat landing but declined and died when the railroad was established through the county, bypassing the river town in favor of Aliceville.

VILLAGE (Old French Village). This early village was just south of U.S. Highway 90 on the Bay Shore Road, approximately 1 mile north of Daphne, in Baldwin County. This area was settled by French and Spanish settlers in the colonial period. A brickyard and pottery plant was established on the site in 1743.[286] Louis Dolive, who established a plantation there in 1803, has, by tradition, been the reputed founder of the Village.[287] It first appeared on the state map in 1839 but disappeared after the Civil War period.

WAKEFIELD. An early county seat, Wakefield was approximately 15 miles south of St. Stephens, in the Sunflower Bend of the Tombigbee River, near McIntosh, in Washington County. This small village was laid out on land that had been claimed by Richard Brashears, and was incorporated in 1805.[288] In that same year the county seat was brought there from McIntosh Bluff, a town 8 miles to the south (see McIntosh Bluff).[289]

The first court was conducted at Wakefield in September, 1805, with Judge Harry Toulmin presiding. In February, 1807, at a cabin in this village the fugitive, Aaron Burr, was recognized, an event which led to his arrest.[290]

In 1809, the county seat was once again removed to McIntosh Bluff, and Wakefield disappeared.[291] A community called New Wakefield, just to the north of Johnson's Creek, appeared on the state map in 1838 and was last listed in 1878.

WASHINGTON. This early Autauga County seat was on the north bank of the Alabama River, just west of Autauga Creek. Autauga County was created by the Alabama Legislature on

November 30, 1818. At first the county business was conducted
"at Jackson's Mill, on the Autauga Creek."[292] The town of Washington was founded in 1817. "W. N. Thompson, a native of England, opened a stock of goods on the Alabama River a few miles
above the mouth of Autauga creek. These goods were purchased
in Milledgeville, Ga., and brought in a two-horse wagon through
an Indian territory from the Ocmulgee. . . . Frank and Thomas
Tarleton are names associated with the early history of the
place."[293]

When Shadrack Mims came to the town in the early 1820s, he
found that "the most conspicuous building that met my view was
a brick building which they called the Court House."[294] He also
stated that a "respectable" building had been erected by Wade H.
Cox, the "founder of the town," and a large store owned by
Pickett and Peck. "There were a good many people in town and
business seemed brisk and lively, more so than in Montgomery."[295] For fifteen years Washington remained the county seat,
but there was much dissatisfaction in the county because of its
location. On December 2, 1830, the state legislature appointed a
commission to select a more suitable site, and Kingston was selected (see Kingston).[296] Washington, in 1879, was reported to
be "all but deserted."[297]

WELLBORN. This early county seat was 12 miles east of
Enterprise and 1 mile east of the Damascus Baptist Church, in
Coffee County. On January 23, 1845, the Alabama Legislature
appointed commissioners to select a county seat within one mile
of the center of the county. The town selected became Wellborn,
named in honor of General William Wellborn. Lots in the town
were sold to the highest bidders with the money used to erect a
courthouse and a jail. These buildings were completed in 1846
from logs cut in the vicinity. There are no records of other buildings, either public or private, ever being erected.[298]

In March, 1851, a fire destroyed the courthouse, and on December 16, the Alabama Legislature authorized a county tax for
the purpose of raising money to rebuild the structure. On January 30, 1852, the legislature passed an act stating that an election
would be held in August to select a permanent site for the county
seat. Three towns competed for the honor—Wellborn, Elba,

and Indigo Head. Elba was chosen, and Wellborn began to die. The post office at Wellborn was closed on August 22, 1866, and the town disappeared from the state map.[299]

WILLIAMSBURG. An early landing, Williamsburg was at Point Clear, on the eastern shore of Mobile Bay, in Baldwin County. In 1800, this land was deeded to Eugenio Lavalle, of Pensacola.[300] A road existed from this point northward to Blakeley and eastward to Perdido Bay as early as 1818, but no town was listed at the site on the map. In 1820, Caleb Dana and Joe Nelson were the first American settlers in the vicinity. The town first appeared on a state map in 1830 and remained on the map until the last quarter of the nineteenth century. The first Point Clear Hotel was erected in 1847, and resort facilities have continued at the site to the present day.[301]

WILLIAMSTON. The oldest town in Barbour County, Williamston was on the headwaters of Choctawhatchee River, approximately 12 miles southwest of Eufaula and 6½ miles southeast of Clayton. The site of this early town was first settled around 1820 by members of the Williams family, who were emigrants from South Carolina. They were soon joined by other families who came to the "Williams' Settlement."[302]

The most prominent of these settlers was Green Beauchamp from Georgia. He established a general store at Williamston and traded with Indians from nearby Eufaula Town. Soon he was accepted by the other settlers as their leader. He also operated a plantation and took part in state politics, serving in the Alabama House of Representatives in 1836–37. Years later he was a member of the Constitutional Convention of 1865.[303]

Williamston existed until the Civil War but vanished soon after the conflict, as the farmers of the area began to trade in Clayton and Eufaula.[304] Even Beauchamp moved away to his plantation at White Oak, where he died on December 11, 1883.[305]

WINTON. This small village was located 4 miles northeast of Somerville, in Morgan County. Although the town of Winton did not exist until the last decade of the nineteenth century, the community had been settled during the period just following the

War of 1812. In the 1890s, a small village was established there. Several stores were erected and a school established. The town was named in honor of an early settler, George Winton. A post office was opened in 1894 but was closed in 1905. Nothing is left to mark the site.[306]

WOOLEY'S SPRINGS. This old resort area was in Section 36, Township 1, Range 3 West, approximately 3 miles from the small town which today bears the same name, in Limestone County. Some authorities stated that Levi Cummings settled on Limestone Creek in the vicinity of the springs in 1807, while others contended that Flud (or Flooda) Mitchell, Sr., John Millhouse, Berry Adams, and Lewis Tillman arrived first in 1808.[307]

The springs were named in honor of Joel Wooley, who had purchased the site in 1820 from Lewis Tillman. The resort was established by a Dr. Millhouse, the grandson of the pioneer John Millhouse, who built a two-story hotel and a cluster of log cabins at the springs in the 1880s. Known for its lively entertainment, the resort continued in operation until the World War I period. The hotel was closed, abandoned, and finally destroyed by fire. The springs were filled in by the overflowing of Little Limestone Creek, and the site is today a wilderness.[308]

YOUNG'S FERRY. This early county seat was near the site of the ancient Indian town of Okfuskee, approximately 40 miles northeast of the junction of the Coosa and Tallapoosa rivers, on the eastern bank of the Tallapoosa, in Tallapoosa County. On March 24, 1832, the Creek Indians ceded lands to the U.S. Government, and a portion of this land became Tallapoosa County on December 18, 1832. Some whites had lived in the area prior to the War of 1812. Young's Ferry was chosen as the first seat of justice for the new county, and remained as such until 1838 when the seat was moved to Dadeville.[309]

NOTES

PART I

1. Thomas McAdory Owen, *History of Alabama and Dictionary of Alabama Biography*, I (Chicago, 1921), p. 1.
2. Ibid., pp. 1–2; Albert Samuel Gatschet, *A Migration Legend of the Creek Indians, With a Linguistic, Historic, and Ethnolographic Introduction*, I (Philadelphia, 1884–1888), p. 125.
3. Randolph F. Blackford, *Fascinating Talladega County: Rich in History and in Legends*, (Talladega, n.d.), p. 64.
4. Owen, I., p. 2.
5. Benjamin Hawkins, *A Sketch of the Creek Country, 1798–1799*, in *Collections of the Georgia Historical Society*, (Savannah, 1848), p. 42.
6. Owen, I, p. 48.
7. H. S. Halbert and T. H. Ball, *The Creek War of 1813 and 1814* (Tuscaloosa: University of Alabama Press, 1969), p. 274.
8. Owen, I, p. 52.
9. Ibid., pp. 52–53; Gatschet, I, pp. 85–89.
10. Owen, I, p. 63; John R. Swanton, *The Indian Tribes of North America* (Washington: Smithsonian Institutional Press, 1971), p. 154. Swanton states that the site was on the north bank of the Alabama River, near the mouth of Autauga Creek.
11. Hawkins, pp. 36–37.
12. Owen, I, p. 63.
13. Ibid.
14. Edward Gaylord Bourne (ed.), *Narratives of the Career of Hernando de Soto*, II (New York, 1904), p. 120.
15. Ibid.
16. Ibid.
17. Ibid., pp. 63–64; Gatschet, p. 393; Hawkins, p. 31.
18. Halbert and Ball, p. 273.
19. Owen, I, p. 64.
20. Hawkins, p. 47.
21. Owen, I, p. 64.
22. Matthew William Clinton, *Tuscaloosa, Alabama: Its Early Days 1816–1865* (Tuscaloosa: The Zonta Club, 1958), p. 8.

23. Owen, I, pp. 154–55.
24. Clinton, pp. 4–7.
25. Ibid., pp. 7–8.
26. Virginia Oden Fosque, "Sumter County Place-Names: A Selection," *Alabama Review*, XIII (January, 1960), p. 54; Owen, I, pp. 163–64.
27. "Historic Sites in Alabama," *Alabama Historical Quarterly*, XV (Spring, 1953), p. 28. Hereafter this source will be cited as "Historic Sites." Owen and other early historians believed the site was on the west side of the Tombigbee River, in southwestern Pickens County.
28. Bourne, II, pp. 129–30.
29. Peter A. Brannon, "The Route of DeSoto from Cosa to Mauvilla," in Marie Bankhead Owen, *The Story of Alabama: A History of the State*, I (New York: Lewis Historical Publishing Company, Inc., 1949), p. 131.
30. Bourne, II, p. 116.
31. "Historic Sites," XV, p. 361.
32. Owen, I, p. 221.
33. Ibid., p. 229; "Historic Sites," XIV, p. 83.
34. Owen, I, p. 229.
35. Daniel Marshall Andrews, "DeSoto's Route from Cofitachequi, in Georgia, to Cosa, in Alabama," in Marie Bankhead Owen, *The Story of Alabama: A History of the State*, I, p. 126. Marie Owen placed the site in Russell County on the west bank of the Chattahoochee River.
36. Bourne, II, pp. 108–09.
37. Owen, I, p. 240.
38. Ibid.
39. Ibid., p. 251.
40. Ibid.
41. Ibid., p. 255.
42. Blackford, pp. 72–73; Halbert and Ball, pp. 275–77.
43. Owen, I, p. 406; Blackford, p. 66.
44. Bourne, II, p. 112.
45. Owen, I, p. 406.
46. Ibid.
47. Ibid., p. 407.
48. Brannon, "Route of DeSoto," p. 525. Earlier it was believed that Coste was on one of the large islands in the Ten Island Shoals on the Coosa River, in St. Clair County (Owen, I, p. 407).
49. Bourne, II, pp. 109–10.
50. Ibid., p. 110.
51. Owen, I, p. 435.
52. Ibid.
53. Ibid.
54. Ibid., p. 438.
55. Ibid. See John P. Brown, *Old Frontiers* (Kingsport: Southern

Publishers, Inc., 1938), pp. 217–19, concerning attacks by the Chicka-
maugas.
    56. "Historic Sites," XIV, p. 246.
    57. Owen, I, p. 500.
    58. Ibid., p. 515.
    59. Ibid.
    60. Hawkins, p. 36.
    61. William Stokes Wyman, "Early Times in the Vicinity of the
Present City of Montgomery," Alabama Historical Society, *Transactions*,
II (1897–1898), p. 31.
    62. Owen, I, p. 559.
    63. "Historic Sites," XIV, p. 259.
    64. Owen, I, p. 639.
    65. Carolyn Thomas Foreman, "John Gunter and His Family,"
Alabama Historical Quarterly, IX (Fall, 1947), p. 413.
    66. Ibid., pp. 412–13; Oliver Day Street, "The Indians of Marshall
County, Alabama," Alabama Historical Society, *Transactions*, IV (1899–
1903), pp. 207–08.
    67. Owen, I, p. 683.
    68. Ibid.; Hawkins, pp. 48–49.
    69. Owen, I,, p. 693.
    70. Ibid.; Hawkins, pp. 44–45.
    71. Halbert and Ball, pp. 271–72.
    72. Owen, I, p. 696.
    73. Bourne, II, pp. 119–20.
    74. Owen, I, p. 697.
    75. Hawkins, p. 32.
    76. Owen, I, p. 697.
    77. "Historic Sites," XV, p. 374.
    78. Owen, I, p. 718; Brannon, "Route of DeSoto," p. 132. Peter
Brannon believed the site was in the forks of Oakmulgee Creek and the
Cahaba River, in Perry County.
    79. Ibid.; Bourne, II, p. 116.
    80. Owen, II, p. 723.
    81. Halbert and Ball, pp. 246–55; Albert James Pickett, *History of
Alabama and Incidentally of Georgia and Mississippi, From the Earliest Period*
(Birmingham: Birmingham Book and Magazine Co. of Birmingham,
Ala., 1962), pp. 574–76. Originally published in 1851.
    82. Owen, II, p. 732.
    83. Hawkins, p. 47.
    84. Halbert and Ball, pp. 273–74.
    85. "Historic Sites," XIV, p. 260.
    86. Owen, II, p. 822; Hawkins, p. 48.
    87. "Historic Sites," XV, p. 352.
    88. Owen, II, p. 825.

89. Ibid.

90. Ibid.

91. Hawkins, p. 55.

92. James D. Horan, (ed.) *The McKenney-Hall Portrait Gallery of American Indians* (New York: Crown Publishers, Inc., 1972), pp. 63–64, 122; Henry Rowe Schoolcraft, *History of the Indian Tribes of the United States: Their Present Conditions and Prospects, and a Sketch of Their Ancient Status* (Philadelphia, 1857), pp. 367–68, 417.

93. "Historic Sites," XIV, p. 255; Brannon, "Route of DeSoto," p. 131. Peter Brannon believed the site was "two miles below Harrell's Station on the Southern Railway, west of Selma and on the Cahaba River."

94. Bourne, II, p. 116.

95. "Historic Sites," XIV, p. 260.

96. Daniel H. Thomas, "Fort Toulouse: The French Outpost at the Alibamos on the Coosa," *Alabama Historical Quarterly*, XXII (Fall, 1960), pp. 146–49.

97. Thomas S. Woodward, *Woodward's Reminiscences of the Creek, or Muscogee Indians* (Montgomery: Barrett & Wimbish, 1859), pp. 36–37; Pickett, pp. 425, 519; Owen, II, p. 746.

98. Owen, II, p. 831.

99. Ibid., p. 832.

100. Ibid., p. 838.

101. Ibid., pp. 838–39.

102. "Historic Sites," XV, p. 358.

103. Ibid.

104. Bourne, II, contains the accounts of the DeSoto Expedition.

105. Pickett, p. 36.

106. Peter J. Hamilton, *Colonial Mobile* (Mobile: The First National Bank of Mobile, 1952), p. 24. This work was originally published in 1897.

107. Ibid., p. 25.

108. Albert Burton Moore, *History of Alabama* (Tuscaloosa: Alabama Book Store, 1951), p. 37.

109. Marie Owen, p. 526.

110. Buddy Smith, "1540 Battle Site Believed Found," *Mobile Press*, March 16, 1973.

111. *Birmingham News*, March 20, 1973.

112. Dr. Edward Palmer, "Alabama Notes Made in 1883–84," *Alabama Historical Quarterly*, XXII (Winter, 1960), pp. 269–70.

113. Ibid.

114. Pickett, p. 36.

115. Bourne, II, p. 124.

116. Ibid., pp. 17–21.

117. Ibid., pp. 21, 76, 127–28.

118. Owen, II, p. 1062.

119. Ibid.

120. James Adair, *The History of the American Indians* (London, 1775), p. 277.

121. Hawkins, p. 35.

122. "Historic Sites," XV, p. 374.

123. Ibid.; Owen, II, pp. 1066–67.

124. Owen, II, p. 1069.

125. Ibid.

126. Hawkins, p. 42.

127. Halbert and Ball, p. 99

128. "Historic Sites," XV, p. 366.

129. Hawkins, pp. 45–46.

130. Owen, II, p. 1088.

131. Pickett, pp. 342–44.

132. Hawkins, p. 39.

133. Owen, II, p. 1088.

134. "Historic Sites," XIV, p. 247.

135. Owen, II, p. 1092.

136. Pickett, pp. 378–81.

137. Owen, II, p. 1092.

138. Ibid.

139. Ibid., p. 1093. See map opposite p. 189 in Hamilton.

140. Ibid.

141. Ibid.

142. Hawkins, p. 37.

143. Owen, II, p. 1094; "Historic Sites," XV, p. 353.

144. Ibid.

145. "Historic Sites," XIV, p. 251.

146. Ibid.

147. Ibid., XV, p. 353.

148. Hawkins, p. 25.

149. Ibid., p. 63.

150. Owen, II, p. 1099. See the John Mitchell map of 1756.

151. Ibid.

152. "Historic Sites," XIV, p. 236.

153. Owen, II, p. 1098.

154. "Historic Sites," XV, p. 54.

155. Brannon, "Route of DeSoto," p. 132.

156. Bourne, II, pp. 122–23.

157. "Historic Sites," XV, p. 359.

158. Ibid.

159. Owen, II, pp. 1227–28.

160. Ibid., p. 1228.

161. "Historic Sites," XV, p. 341.

162. Ibid., pp. 341–42.

163. Hawkins, pp. 34–35.

164. Pickett, pp. 618–22.

165. "Historic Sites," XV, p. 354.
166. Owen, II, p. 1228.
167. "Historic Sites," XV, p. 367.
168. Ibid.
169. Hawkins, p. 48.
170. Blackford, p. 30; Owen, II, p. 1288.
171. Owen, II, p. 1288.
172. Pickett, p. 554; Halbert and Ball, p. 269; Blackford, pp. 18–19;
E. Grace Jemison, *Historic Tales of Talladega* (Montgomery: Paragon Press, 1959), pp. 35–37.
173. Pickett, pp. 554–55; Jemison, p. 37.
174. "Historic Sites," XV, p. 50.
175. Bourne, II, p. 111.
176. Brannon, p. 129.
177. Bourne, II, p. 113.
178. "Historic Sites," XIV, pp. 231–32.
179. Ibid.; Pickett, p. 553.
180. Owen, II, p. 1289.
181. Ibid.
182. Hawkins, pp. 26–27.
183. Owen, II, p. 1289.
184. "Historic Sites," XIV, p. 256.
185. Bourne, II, p. 115.
186. Ibid., p. 116.
187. "Historic Sites," XIV, p. 80.
188. Hawkins, p. 26.
189. Owen, II, p. 1303.
190. Ibid.
191. Hawkins, p. 38.
192. Pickett, pp. 470–71.
193. Andrews, p. 128.
194. Bourne, II, p. 112.
195. Brannon, p. 130; "Historic Sites," XV, p. 342.
196. Bourne, II, pp. 114–15.
197. Owen, II, p. 1304.
198. Ibid., p. 1312.
199. Horan, pp. 134–35; Woodward, pp. 97–98; Halbert and Ball, pp. 92–93, 128–29, 159–60, 300–01.
200. Owen, II, p. 1320.
201. Ibid.; "Historic Sites," XIV, p. 260.
202. "Historic Sites," XIV, p. 261.
203. Ibid.
204. Hawkins, pp. 27, 51–52.
205. Halbert and Ball, p. 79.
206. Woodward, pp. 84, 95; Pickett, pp. 514–15.

207. Pickett, pp. 515, 520.
208. Owen, II, p. 1332.
209. "Historic Sites," XIV, p. 235.
210. Owen, II, p. 1332.
211. Halbert and Ball, p. 271.
212. "Historic Sites," XV, p. 374.
213. Bourne, II, p. 117.
214. Owen, II, p. 1372.
215. Ibid.
216. Hawkins, p. 43.
217. "Historic Sites," XIV, p. 261.
218. Owen, II, p. 1398.
219. "Historic Sites," XIV, p. 252.
220. Owen, II, p. 1392.
221. Ibid., pp. 1406–07.
222. Ibid.; Brown, p. 175.
223. "Historic Sites," XV, p. 38; Owen, II, p. 1410. Owen placed the site at the falls of Big Uchee Creek, at Perry's Ford, 6 miles northeast of Seale, in Russell County.
224. For material on the "Green Corn Dance" see Hawkins, pp. 77–78; Pickett, pp. 101–04.
225. Owen, II, pp. 1410–11.
226. Ibid., p. 1421. Owen listed 5 sites as "Yufaula."
227. Hawkins, p. 42.
228. "Historic Sites," XV, p. 42.
229. Ibid.
230. Ibid., pp. 30–31.
231. Swanton, p. 173.
232. "Historic Sites," XV, pp. 30–31.

PART II

1. "Historic Sites," XIV, p. 235.
2. Owen, I, p. 614.
3. Pickett, p. 579.
4. Ibid.
5. Owen, I, p. 614.
6. H. M. King, "Historical Sketches of Macon County," *Alabama Historical Quarterly*, XVIII (Summer, 1956), pp. 190–91, originally published in *The Macon Mail*, Tuskegee, February 9, 1881.
7. Peter A. Brannon, "Lewis' Tavern at Fort Bainbridge," *Alabama Historical Quarterly*, XVII (1955), pp. 78–79.
8. "Historic Sites," XIV, pp. 84–85.
9. Pickett, p. 619.

10. Rev. C. E. Crenshaw, "Indian Massacres in Butler County in 1818," Alabama Historical Society, *Transactions*, IV (1899–1903), pp. 99–100; Pickett, pp. 618–20.

11. Pickett, pp. 621–22.

12. L. J. Newcomb Comings and Martha M. Albers, *A Brief History of Baldwin County* (Fairhope: Baldwin County Historical Society, 1928), p. 37.

13. John H. Foshee, "Alabama's Forgotten Battles: Fort Blakeley and Spanish Fort," *Birmingham News Magazine*, December 5, 1965.

14. Robert Underwood Johnson and Clarence Clough (eds.), *Battles and Leaders of the Civil War*, IV (New York: Thomas Yoseloff, Inc., 1956), pp. 410–11. Hereafter this source with be referred to as *Battles and Leaders*.

15. Halbert and Ball, p. 114.

16. Rev. T. H. Ball, *A Glance Into the Great South-East, or, Clarke County, Alabama, and Its Surroundings, From 1540 to 1877* (Grove Hill, privately published, 1882), p. 495.

17. Halbert and Ball, p. 113.

18. Ibid.

19. "Historic Sites," XIV, p. 231. For the heroic actions of Chinnabee, see Blackford, p. 18; Jemison, p. 31; Woodward, p. 77.

20. W. Stuart Harris, *Southern Historical Records*, XV (original manuscript, 1966), p. 1.

21. Halbert and Ball, pp. 241–42.

22. Major Howell Tatum, "Topographical Notes and Observations on the Alabama River, August, 1814," Alabama Historical Society, *Transactions*, II (1897–1898), pp. 159–60.

23. Caldwell Delaney, *The Story of Mobile* (Mobile: Gill Printing Company, 1953), p. 26.

24. Hamilton, pp. 86–87, 90.

25. Ibid., pp. 153–54.

26. Ibid., p. 217.

27. Ibid., pp. 412–13.

28. Ibid., p. 481.

29. "Historic Sites," XIV, p. 262.

30. Robert Leslie Scribner, "A Short History of Brewton, Alabama," *Alabama Historical Quarterly*, XI (1949), pp. 17–27.

31. "Historic Sites," XIV, p. 239.

32. Ibid. For excellent accounts of the battle of Burnt Corn Creek, see Pickett, pp. 521–25 and Halbert and Ball, pp. 125–42.

33. "Historic Sites," XIV, p. 85.

34. J. F. H. Claiborne, *Life and Times of General Sam. Dale, The Mississippi Partisan* (New York: Harper and Brothers, 1860), p. 170.

35. "Historic Sites," XV, p. 43.

36. Ibid., pp. 43–44.

37. Ibid., p. 51.
38. Pickett, p. 552.
39. "Historic Sites," XV, p. 41.
40. Halbert and Ball, p. 246.
41. Ibid., p. 112; also see the map on the opposite page.
42. Ibid.
43. Ibid., p. 113.
44. Ibid., p. 108, with map on opposite page.
45. Claiborne, pp. 116–17. Sam Dale stated that he took charge of this fort soon after the battle of Burnt Corn Creek, at which time it contained 15 families.
46. "Historic Sites," XIV, p. 239.
47. Owen, II, pp. 1225–26; T. J. Krouse, "Clarke County Salt Works," *Alabama Historical Quarterly*, XX (Spring, 1958) pp. 95–100.
48. "Historic Sites," XV, pp. 39–40.
49. Thomas Smith Malone, "Scraps Relating To The Early History of Limestone County," *Alabama Historical Quarterly*, XVIII (Fall, 1956), pp. 312, 314–15, originally published in *Athens Post*, March 18, 23, 1867.
50. "Historic Sites," XV, p. 44.
51. Pickett, pp. 584, 586.
52. This site is marked on most modern-day maps.
53. Pickett, p. 593.
54. Ibid., pp. 593–95.
55. Halbert and Ball, p. 112.
56. Blackford, p. 47.
57. Ibid., pp. 47–48; Jemison, pp. 29–30.
58. Blackford, pp. 49–50.
59. Halbert and Ball, p. 115.
60. Ibid., p. 197.
61. "Historic Sites," XV, p. 53.
62. Hamilton, p. 53. M. Penicaut stated that the work on this fort was started in 1701.
63. M. Penicaut, "Annals of Louisiana, From 1698 to 1722," *Alabama Historical Quarterly*, V (Fall, 1943), pp. 291–92; also see Hamilton, p. 53.
64. Hamilton, p. 85.
65. Halbert and Ball, p. 114.
66. Ibid.
67. Ibid., pp. 219–21.
68. "Historic Sites," XIV, p. 240.
69. Halbert and Ball, p. 110.
70. Ibid., pp. 110–11.
71. Ibid., p. 197.
72. Claiborne, pp. 116–17.
73. "Historic Sites," XIV, p. 78.

74. Pickett, pp. 528–29.
75. Ibid., p. 530.
76. James F. Doster, "Letters Relating to the Tragedy of Fort Mims: August–September, 1813," *Alabama Review,* XIV (October, 1961), pp. 272–73.
77. For excellent accounts of the massacre at Fort Mims, see Pickett, pp. 528–43; Halbert and Ball, pp. 143–76.
78. Laurence H. Marks, "Fort Mims: A Challenge," *Alabama Review,* XVIII (October, 1965), p. 277.
79. "Baldwin's Ft. Mims in National Register," *Birmingham News,* September 27, 1972; Frank Sikora, "Excavators Mark 160th Anniversary of Massacre," *Birmingham News,* August 12, 1973.
80. This site appears on most modern-day maps.
81. Peter Brannon (ed.), "Some Early Fort Mitchell References," *Alabama Historical Quarterly,* XXI (1959), pp. 3–5.
82. Owen, III, p. 432; Nella J. Chambers, "The Creek Indian Factory at Fort Mitchell," *Alabama Historical Quarterly,* XXI (1959), p. 15.
83. Chambers, p. 26.
84. William B. Collins, "The Crawford-Burnside Duel," *Gulf States Historical Magazine,* II (July, 1903), p. 54.
85. Peter Brannon, "Woolfolk-Camp Duel," *Alabama Historical Quarterly,* XXI (1959), pp. 111–12.
86. Owen, I, p. 615.
87. Ibid.
88. Pickett, p. 545.
89. Hamilton, p. 400.
90. Owen, II, p. 1061.
91. Ibid.
92. Ibid., pp. 1061–62.
93. Ibid., p. 1093.
94. Ibid., pp. 1093–94.
95. Halbert and Ball, p. 108.
96. Ibid., pp. 108, 164.
97. Ibid., p. 244.
98. See map of Mobile Bay in *Battles and Leaders,* IV, p. 384.
99. Ibid., pp. 400, 409.
100. Gordon T. Chappell, "Alabama Historical Association, Announcement of 1960 Pilgrimage," letter to members, dated October 18, 1960.
101. Pickett, p. 417.
102. Hamilton, p. 377.
103. George S. Gaines, "Gaines' Reminiscences," *Alabama Historical Quarterly,* XXVI (Fall and Winter, 1964), pp. 140–41.
104. Halbert and Ball, pp. 216–17.
105. "Historic Sites," XV, p. 355.

106. Peter Brannon, "Russell County Place Names," *Alabama Historical Quarterly*, XXI (1959), p. 101.

107. Ibid.

108. Halbert and Ball, p. 111.

109. Ibid.

110. Ibid., pp. 177–81; Pickett, pp. 544–45.

111. Halbert and Ball, pp. 184–99; Pickett, pp. 545–46.

112. Hamilton, p. 316.

113. Ibid., pp. 316–17.

114. *Battles and Leaders*, IV, pp. 411–12; James Robert Maxwell, *Autobiography of James Robert Maxwell* (New York: Greenberg, Publisher, 1926), pp. 280–82.

115. Owen, II, p. 1272.

116. Jack D. L. Holmes (ed.), "Fort Stoddart in 1799: Seven Letters of Captain Bartholomew Schaumburgh," *Alabama Historical Quarterly*, XXVI (Fall, 1964), pp. 231–52.

117. Pickett, p. 494; Ball, p. 84.

118. Owen, II, p. 1272.

119. Ibid.

120. "Historic Sites," XV, p. 358.

121. Jemison, pp. 35–37.

122. The author visited this site in 1963.

123. John Allan Wyeth, *That Devil Forrest: Life of General Nathan Bedford Forrest* (New York: Harper & Brothers, 1959), pp. 426–33.

124. Ibid., pp. 434–35.

125. Robert Selph Henry (ed.), *As They Saw Forrest* (Jackson: McCowat-Mercer Press, Inc., 1956), p. 200.

126. The author made extensive investigations in this area in 1967.

127. Hamilton, pp. 127, 195–96.

128. Ibid., p. 222; Robert R. Rea, "The Trouble at Tombeckby," *Alabama Review*, XXI (January, 1968), pp. 21–39.

129. Hamilton, pp. 246, 259.

130. Gaines, p. 177.

131. Ibid., pp. 178–80.

132. The author visited this site several times in 1965.

133. Thomas, p. 147.

134. Ibid., p. 150.

135. Ibid., pp. 150–51.

136. Ibid., pp. 158–61.

137. Ibid., pp. 203–06.

138. For other references on Fort Toulouse, see Peter Hamilton's *Colonial Mobile;* Penicaut's *Annals of Louisiana;* and Lucille Griffith, "South Carolina and Fort Alabama, 1714–1763," *Alabama Review*, XII (October, 1959), pp. 258–71.

139. Halbert and Ball, pp. 112–13.

140. Ibid.
141. Ibid., p. 219.
142. "Historic Sites," XIV, p. 234.
143. *Battles and Leaders*, IV, p. 761.
144. Ibid.
145. Halbert and Ball, p. 112.
146. Pickett, p. 526.
147. Blackford, p. 71. Though the actual site is inundated, a historic marker and the graves of some of Jackson's men are still located near the site.
148. Pickett, p. 587.
149. Ibid., p. 592.

PART III

1. Winston Smith, "Early History of Demopolis," *Alabama Review*, XVIII (April, 1965), p. 85.
2. Ibid., p. 86.
3. Hamner Cobbs, "Geography of the Vine and Olive Colony," *Alabama Review*, XIV (April, 1961), pp. 85–86.
4. Ibid., p. 87; Winston Smith, p. 85; O. B. Emerson, "The Bonapartist Exiles in Alabama," *Alabama Review*, XI (April, 1958), p. 140.
5. Gaius Whitfield, Jr., "The French Grant in Alabama, A History of the Founding of Demopolis," Alabama Historical Society, *Transactions*, (1899–1903), p. 347.
6. Pickett, pp. 626–27; Whitfield, pp. 351–52.
7. W. Stuart Harris, *Southern Historical Records,* IV, XIII, XIV (unpublished manuscripts, 1960–1964). These volumes contain research materials taken from primary sources.
8. T. G. Bradford's "Map of Alabama" was the first map to show the site.
9. Carl Elliott (ed.), *Annals of Northwest Alabama,* I, (Tuscaloosa, 1958), pp. 161–62.
10. Robert A. Russell, "Gold Mining in Alabama Before 1860," *Alabama Review*, X (January, 1957), pp. 5–9; J. T. Langley, "Alabama's Gold Rush Was A Real Lulu," *Birmingham News Magazine,* May 5, 1963, p. 14.
11. Russell, p. 10.
12. George I. Adams, "A Century of Gold Mining in Alabama," *Alabama Historical Quarterly,* I (Fall, 1930), pp. 272–73.
13. The author investigated this site during the early 1960s, while gathering materials for his *Southern Historical Records.*
14. Emerson, p. 140.
15. Harris, IV (1960), p. 159.

16. Owen, II, p. 992.
17. Ibid.
18. Nina Leftwich, *Two Hundred Years At Muscle Shoals* (Birmingham, 1935), pp. 40, 42.
19. Ibid., p. 40.
20. Ibid.
21. James Edmonds Saunders, *Early Settlers of Alabama* (New Orleans, 1899), p. 433.
22. Leftwich, p. 42.
23. Owen, II, p. 800.
24. Ibid., I, p. 698.
25. T. G. Bradford, "Map of Alabama," dated 1838.
26. Owen, I, p. 72.
27. From original documents in the author's private collection; also Owen, I, pp. 127–28.
28. James F. Sulzby, Jr., *Birmingham, As It Was, In Jackson County* (Birmingham, 1944), pp. 1–25.
29. James F. Sulzby, Jr., *Historic Alabama Hotels and Resorts* (University, 1960), p. 52. Other notes pertaining to Sulzby are from this volume.
30. Ibid., p. 54.
31. Ibid., p. 58.
32. Hamilton, pp. 404–07, 497.
33. Ibid., p. 449.
34. Ibid.
35. "Soil and Climate of the American Territories," *Port Folio*, series 5, IV (October, 1817), pp. 325–32.
36. Clarence Edwin Carter (ed.), *The Territorial Papers of the United States*, XVIII (Washington, 1952), pp. 497–99.
37. Harris, XIX (1971), pp. 12–15. These materials were abstracted from the original documents by the author.
38. Ibid., p. 15.
39. Ibid.; Comings and Albers, pp. 44–45.
40. John Melish, "Map of Alabama, Constructed From the Surveys in the General Land Office and Other Documents," dated 1818.
41. Harris, XXIV (1969), p. 127.
42. Ibid.
43. Willis Brewer, *Alabama: Her History, Resources, War Record, and Public Men* (Montgomery, 1872), p. 235.
44. Peel E. Sannoner, "Map of the Late Surveys in the Northern District of the Alabama Territory," dated 1817.
45. Harris, XXIX (1970), p. 196.
46. Elliott, I, p. 163.
47. Ibid., II, pp. 79–84.

48. Ibid., I, p. 163.
49. Owen, I, p. 186.
50. Ibid.; Carter, XVIII, pp. 436–37, 447–48; Anna M. Gayle Fry, *Memories of Old Cahaba* (privately published, 1905), p. 13.
51. Fry, pp. 13–14; Owen, I, pp. 203–04.
52. Owen, I, p. 204.
53. Fry, pp. 14–17.
54. Peter A. Brannon, "The Cahawba Military Prison, 1863–1865," *Alabama Review*, III (July, 1950), pp. 163–73.
55. Owen, I, p. 188.
56. Hugh W. Sparrow, "Once Busy State Capital: Rivers, Rerouting Railroads Reduce Cahaba to Ghost Town," *Birmingham News*, July 17, 1960.
57. W. Stuart Harris, *A Short History of Marion, Perry County, Alabama, Its Homes and Its Buildings* (Marion, 1970), p. 1.
58. Ibid.; S. A. Townes, "The History of Marion: Sketches of Life in Perry County, Alabama," *Alabama Historical Quarterly*, XIV (1952), p. 184.
59. Harris, *Short History of Marion*, p. 1; Townes, pp. 184–86.
60. Peel E. Sannoner, "Map of the Late Surveys in the Northern District of the Alabama Territory," dated 1817.
61. V. Gayle Snedecor, *A Directory of Greene County For 1855–56* (Mobile, 1856), p. 60.
62. *Alabama Beacon*, Greensboro, August 26, 1848. All known issues of this paper have been abstracted by the author in *Southern Historical Records*, XVIII (1968).
63. Ibid.
64. *Alabama Beacon*, Greensboro, February 29, 1868.
65. Owen, I, p. 196; Brewer, p. 578.
66. Harris, X (1961), p. 146; Ethel Armes, *The Story of Coal and Iron in Alabama* (Birmingham, 1910), p. 44; B. E. Grace, "Early History: Jefferson County As It Was In By-gone Days," *Jefferson County and Birmingham, Alabama* (Birmingham, 1887), p. 55.
67. Ibid.; also see Virginia Pounds Brown and Jane Porter Nabers (ed.), "Mary Gordon Duffee's 'Sketches of Alabama,' " *Alabama Review*, IX (April, 1956), pp. 149–51.
68. Peel E. Sannoner, "Map of the Late Surveys in the Northern District of the Alabama Territory," dated 1817.
69. John Knox, *A History of Morgan County, Alabama* (Decatur, 1966), pp. 44–45.
70. E. G. Richards, "Reminiscenses of the Early Days in Chambers County," *Alabama Historical Quarterly*, IV (Fall, 1942), pp. 417–19; Nella J. Chambers, "Early Days in East Alabama," *Alabama Review*, XIII (July, 1960), pp. 179–80.

71. Richards, pp. 421–22; Chambers, pp. 180–81.
72. Sulzby, pp. 93–94; Jemison, pp. 187–88.
73. Sulzby, p. 94.
74. Ibid., pp. 94–96.
75. Russell, p. 10.
76. Jack Hopper, "There's Gold in the Talladega Mountains—But Not Enough To Make It Worthwhile," *Birmingham News,* September 15, 1965.
77. Brewer, pp. 434–35.
78. "Soil and Climate of the American Territories," p. 330.
79. Justus Wyman, "Fort Claiborne," *Alabama Historical Quarterly,* XIX (Summer, 1957), p. 217.
80. Owen, II, p. 1270.
81. Peter A. Brannon, "LaFayette's Visit To Claiborne," *Alabama Historical Quarterly,* XIX (Summer, 1957), p. 260.
82. Caroline Gaillard Hurtel, *The River Plantation of Thomas and Marianne Gaillard, 1832–1850* (Mobile, 1959), p. 9.
83. Brewer, p. 435.
84. Owen, I, p. 269.
85. Ibid.
86. Ibid., pp. 269–70.
87. Ibid., II, pp. 954–55; Brewer, pp. 383–84.
88. Leftwich, pp. 19–23.
89. Dawson A. Phelps, "Colbert Ferry," *Alabama Historical Quarterly,* XXV (Fall, 1963), pp. 206–12.
90. John Knox, "Countrymen Tied 'Pioneers' To Indians, Helped Change the Face of the Frontier," *The Decatur Daily,* November 29, 1964.
91. Edward C. Betts, *Early History of Huntsville, Alabama, 1804 to 1870* (Montgomery, 1916), p. 6.
92. B. Palmer Lewis, *John Hardie of Thornhill, His Life, Letters and Times* (New York, 1928), p. 126.
93. W. Stanley Hoole, *Alias Simon Suggs: The Life and Times of Johnson Jones Hooper* (University, 1952), pp. 31–34.
94. Sidney E. Norse and Samuel Breese, "Map of Alabama," 1842.
95. Pickett stated that the body was first buried on the battlefield and the ground was then burned over to conceal the site. Pickett, p. 592. In 1972 the remains of the hero were buried with honors at the Horseshoe Bend National Military Park.
96. Harris, XXVI (1972), p. 82.
97. Armes, p. 44; W. Stanley Hoole (ed.), "Elyton, Alabama, and the Connecticut Asylum: The Letters of William H. Ely, 1820–1821," *Alabama Review,* III (January, 1950), pp. 36–39, 56.
98. Armes, p. 44; Brown and Nabers, IX (July, 1956), pp. 224–26, 228–32.

99. Hoole, "Elyton," p. 58.
100. Brown and Nabers, IX (July, 1956), pp. 231–32.
101. Anson West, *History of Methodism in Alabama* (Nashville, 1893), pp. 120–121; "Walker Memorial Will Observe 141st Birthday," *Birmingham News*, May 16, 1959.
102. Rhoda Coleman Ellison, *History and Bibliography of Alabama Newspapers in the Nineteenth Century* (University, 1954), p. 50.
103. Ibid.
104. Harris, X (1961), pp. 163–64.
105. *Battles and Leaders*, IV, pp. 759–61; Armes, pp. 189–90.
106. Malcolm C. McMillan, *Yesterday's Birmingham* (Miami, 1975), pp. 18–19.
107. Snedecor, p. 63.
108. Ibid., pp. 61–62.
109. Gravestone in the cemetery at Erie.
110. Harris, XVIII (1968), pp. 120–39.
111. Snedecor, pp. 65–66.
112. *Alabama Beacon*, Greensboro, November 17, 1849.
113. Ibid., July 29, 1848.
114. Snedecor, p. 63.
115. Nelson F. Smith, "History of Pickens County, Ala.," in Elliott, I, p. 17.
116. Ibid., p. 89.
117. Stuart Covington, "Town Moved To Railroad Tracks," *Birmingham News*, September 15, 1971.
118. Elliott, II, pp. 259–60.
119. William R. Smith, Sr., *Reminiscences of a Long Life* (Washington, 1889), pp. 31–44.
120. Elliott, I, p. 164.
121. Ibid., p. 179.
122. Ibid., p. 164.
123. W. M. Massey, "Legendary Falls Will Drown In Own Water," *Birmingham News Magazine*, February 12, 1961.
124. J. W. Colton, "Map of Alabama," dated 1853.
125. Owen, I, p. 181.
126. T. G. Bradford, "Map of Alabama," dated 1838.
127. "Gray's Atlas Map of Alabama," dated 1874.
128. Peter A. Brannon, "Old Glennville: An Early Center of East Alabama Culture," *Alabama Review*, XI (October, 1958), pp. 255–56.
129. Ibid., p. 256; Brewer, pp. 511–12.
130. Brannon, p. 263.
131. Ralph Hammond, *Ante-Bellum Mansions of Alabama* (New York, 1951), pp. 179–82.
132. Brannon, pp. 257–58.
133. Ibid., pp. 260–61.

134. Anne Kendrick Walker, *Backtracking in Barbour County: A Narrative of the Last Alabama Frontier* (Richmond, 1941), pp. 152–53.

135. Russell, p. 11.

136. Ibid.

137. The population of Goldville in 1973 was reported to be 21 persons. Plans are now under way to make the area a tourist attraction.

138. Elliott, II, pp. 264–65.

139. Owen, I, p. 317.

140. Benjamin Franklin Riley, *History of Conecuh County, Alabama* (Columbus, 1881), p. 29.

141. Ibid., pp. 43–44.

142. Ibid., pp. 44–46; Owen, I, p. 317.

143. Brown and Nabers, IX (October, 1956), p. 271.

144. Harris, X (1961), p. 20. This date can be found in the *Sale of Public Lands, Jefferson County, Alabama,* in the county records.

145. Brown and Nabers, IX (October, 1956), pp. 271–72.

146. Armes, pp. 49–50.

147. Brown and Nabers, IX (October, 1956), p. 271.

148. Ibid., pp. 272–73; Armes, pp. 48–49.

149. Ibid., p. 275.

150. *Alabama Beacon,* Greensboro, July 29, 1848.

151. Ibid., January 12, 1850.

152. Snedecor, p. 68.

153. Ford Cook, "Scenes Of Century Ago Visualized From Trace Of Baldwin Settlement," *Mobile Press Register,* January 22, 1961.

154. Ibid.

155. John B. Weaver, "Fact and Fiction of the Free State of Winston," in Elliott, I, pp. 174–81.

156. Moore, p. 543.

157. Weaver, pp. 177–78; Milo B. Howard (ed.), "Governor John Gill Shorter Executive Papers," *Alabama Historical Quarterly,* XXIII (Fall, 1961), pp. 278–84.

158. John Cargile, "In Winston County Tiny, Run-down Jail Symbolizes Bloody Era," *Birmingham News,* August 17, 1969.

159. Thomas F. Hill, "Independence, Ala.: Town Quite Busy Going Nowhere," *Birmingham News,* July 2, 1963.

160. Armes, p. 316; Blackford, pp. 22–23.

161. Jemison, p. 192.

162. Ibid.

163. Owen, II, p. 1278.

164. Harris, XII (1966), p. 133.

165. Armes, pp. 178–79.

166. Blackford, p. 14.

167. Jemison, p. 192.

168. Ibid.; Armes, p. 316.

169. Ibid., pp. 192–93.
170. Owen, II, p. 888; Brown and Nabers, IX (April, 1956), p. 140. Duffee stated that Jones settled in Jefferson County in 1816.
171. Harris, X (1961), p. 125. This information was obtained from the original land records of Jefferson County.
172. *Jones Valley Times*, Elyton, July 1, 1854.
173. Harris, X (1961), pp. 14, 41, 171.
174. Ibid., pp. 150–64.
175. Owen, II, p. 1132.
176. Armes, pp. 334–35.
177. John Hardy, "History of Autauga County," *Daily State Sentinel,* Selma, August 10, 1867.
178. Owen, IV, p. 1668.
179. In 1867, John Hardy stated that Kingston's population consisted "of the county officers, a tavern-keeper, grocery-keeper and one physician, with their respective families." Hardy, *Daily State Sentinel,* Selma, August 10, 1867.
180. John Knox, "Roses Reveal Site of the Lost Academy, LaGrange Was An Active and Bustling Town," *The Decatur Daily,* November 15, 1964.
181. Ibid.
182. Ibid.; Owen, II, pp. 837–38.
183. Ibid.
184. Ibid.
185. Morse and Breese, "Map of Alabama," dated 1842.
186. George Evans Brewer, "History of Coosa County," *Alabama Historical Quarterly,* IV (Spring, 1942), p. 37.
187. Ibid., p. 38.
188. Ibid., p. 40.
189. Elliott, II, pp. 258–59.
190. Owen, II, pp. 1178–79; Harris, XXIX (1972), p. 198.
191. Theodore Bowling Pearson, "Early Settlement Around Historic McIntosh Bluff: Alabama's First County Seat," *Alabama Review,* XXIII (October, 1970), pp. 245–46.
192. Ibid., pp. 246–47.
193. Ibid., pp. 248–50, 253; Pickett, pp. 474–75; Owen, II, p. 918.
194. Pearson, p. 254.
195. Ibid., pp. 254–55.
196. Ibid., p. 255. In 1970 the residents of this area, hoping for a prosperous future because of the construction of the Tennessee-Tombigbee waterway, voted to incorporate.
197. Jemison, pp. 71–72.
198. Ibid., pp. 72–73; Blackford, pp. 60–61.
199. Jemison, p. 73; Blackford, p. 61.

200. For references on the life of John Hardie, see B. Palmer Lewis, *John Hardie of Thornhill, His Life, Letters and Times* (New York, 1928).

201. Anne Newport Royall, *Letters From Alabama, 1817–1822* (University, 1969), pp. 134–36.

202. Ibid., pp. 136–38.

203. Owen, II, p. 856.

204. From gravestones in the Old Memphis Cemetery.

205. Stuart Covington, "Memphis On Tombigbee—Once Thriving Port Now Gone," *Birmingham News*, July 31, 1960.

206. Ibid.

207. T. G. Bradford, "Map of Alabama," dated 1838.

208. Owen, I, p. 429; Brewer, pp. 201–02.

209. Comings and Albers, pp. 56–58.

210. T. G. Bradford, "Map of Alabama," dated 1838.

211. Ibid.

212. Ibid.

213. Elliott, II, p. 260.

214. Clinton, p. 43; see W. Stanley Hoole (ed.), "Elyton, Alabama, And The Connecticut Asylum: The Letters of William H. Ely, 1820–1821," *Alabama Review*, III (January, 1950), pp. 36–69, for additional information.

215. Clinton, p. 43.

216. William R. Smith, Sr., p. 25.

217. Ibid.

218. Ibid., p. 26; Clinton, pp. 54–55.

219. Leftwich, pp. 38–39.

220. Jemison, pp. 193–94.

221. Ibid.

222. Sulzby, pp. 194–95.

223. Jemison, p. 194.

224. Ibid.; Sulzby, p. 195.

225. J. W. Colton, "Map of Alabama," dated 1853.

226. Henry B. Foster, *History of the Tuscaloosa County Baptist Association, 1834–1934* (Tuscaloosa, 1934), p. 87.

227. Owen, II, p. 942.

228. Loy Mitchell, "A Glimpse of Early Marion County," in Elliott, I, p. 217.

229. Armes, p. 151.

230. Frank Sikora, "When Mines Close Few Folks Stay in Empty Towns," *Birmingham News*, February 16, 1969; Larry Corcoran, "Piper: Mere Ghost Town," *Birmingham News*, June 23, 1967.

231. Hamilton, pp. 171–72.

232. Ibid., p. 518.

233. Delaney, p. 89.

234. Bert Neville, *Directory of River Packets in the Mobile-Alabama-Warrior-Tombigbee Trades, 1818–1932* (Selma, 1962), p. 146.

235. Ibid., pp. 21, 25.

236. Selma and Dallas County Sesquicentennial Committee, *150 Years, Selma and Dallas County*, p. 32.

237. The author has visited the site many times in company with Laird Love, the property owner.

238. Ibid.; interview with the late John Laird.

239. Jemison, pp. 194–95.

240. Ibid.

241. Owen, I, p. 686; W. L. Andrews, "Early History of Southeast Alabama," *Alabama Historical Quarterly*, X (1948), pp. 100–01.

242. Owen, I, p. 443.

243. Ibid., p. 444.

244. Hamilton, pp. 283–84.

245. Ibid., p. 511; Jack D. L. Holmes, "Notes On The Spanish Fort San Esteban De Tombecbe," *Alabama Review*, XVIII (October, 1965), p. 282.

246. Holmes, p. 286.

247. Ibid., p. 289.

248. Father Aloysius Plaisance, "The Choctaw Trading House, 1803–1822," *Alabama Historical Quarterly*, XVI (Fall and Winter, 1954), p. 395; George S. Gaines, "Gaines' Reminiscences," *Alabama Historical Quarterly*, XXVI (Fall and Winter, 1964), p. 139.

249. Gaines, pp. 140–41.

250. Ibid., p. 154.

251. Kirby to Jefferson, May 1, 1804, in Carter, V, pp. 322–23.

252. W. Stuart Harris (ed.), *Diaries of the American Frontier* (unpublished manuscript, 1967), pp. 94, 100. The original diary came from Lorenzo Dow, *The Dealings of God, Man, And The Devil; As Exemplified In The Life, Experience, And Travels of Lorenzo Dow, In a Period Of Over Half A Century* (St. Louis, 1850).

253. Owen, II, p. 1224.

254. Mary Welsh, "Reminiscences of Old Saint Stephens, of More Than Sixty-five Years Ago," Alabama Historical Society, *Transactions*, III (1898–1899), p. 221.

255. "The Spanish Evacuation Centennial, St. Stephens, Alabama, May 6, 1899," Alabama Historical Society, *Transactions*, III (1898–1899), pp. 227–36.

256. Sulzby, pp. 209–10.

257. Ibid., pp. 210–12.

258. Ibid., pp. 212–14.

259. Ibid., pp. 214–17.

260. Brewer, p. 518.

261. Harris, XXIX (1972), p. 233.

262. Owen, II, p. 1242.

263. Peel E. Sannoner, "Map of the Late Surveys in the Northern District of the Alabama Territory," dated 1817; Leftwich, p. 42.

264. Leftwich, pp. 43–44.

265. Riley, pp. 44–45; Owen, I, p. 317.

266. Ibid., p. 45.

267. Ibid., pp. 45–46; Owen, I, p. 315.

268. Ibid.

269. Ibid., pp. 146–47.

270. Ibid., pp. 173–74; Owen, I, p. 317.

271. Owen, I, p. 315.

272. *Alabama Beacon*, Greensboro, October 27, 1836; Harris, XVIII (1968), p. 144.

273. Snedecor, pp. 67–68.

274. John Knox, *A History of Morgan County, Alabama* (Decatur, 1966), pp. 92–93.

275. Ibid.

276. Knox, p. 81.

277. Elliott, I, p. 181.

278. John Knox, "Ancient Groves Hide Dramas of the Past, Old Soldiers and Governors Lived At Triana," *The Decatur Daily*, September 16, 1964.

279. Owen, II, p. 1403. Owen stated that Upper Peach Tree retained its name until 1835, when the landing was purchased by several individuals. The name was then changed to Clifton.

280. Sulzby, pp. 90–92.

281. Ibid.

282. Ibid.

283. Shadrack Mims, "History of Autauga County," *Alabama Historical Quarterly*, VIII (Fall, 1946), p. 243.

284. Ibid., p. 245.

285. Ibid., p. 252; see John Hardy, "History of Autauga County," *Alabama Historical Quarterly*, III (Spring, 1941), p. 105.

286. Hamilton, p. 516.

287. Ibid., p. 514; Comings and Albers, pp. 49–50; Walker D. Wallace, "Old Hickory Camped Here," *Birmingham News Magazine*, August 14, 1960.

288. Owen, II, p. 1382.

289. Pearson, p. 254.

290. Pickett, pp. 488–502.

291. Pearson, p. 254.

292. Owen, I, p. 77.

293. "Then And Now: Early History of Autauga Written By One of Its Oldest Citizens," *Prattville Progress*, May 3, 1885.

294. Mims, p. 241.

295. Ibid., pp. 241–42.
296. Owen, I, p. 77.
297. Hardy, p. 103.
298. Harris, XXIX (1972), p. 261; Owen, I, pp. 297–98; Brewer, pp. 185–86.
299. Ibid.
300. Hamilton, p. 516.
301. Sulzby, p. 136.
302. Walker, p. 17.
303. Ibid., pp. 17–19.
304. Ibid., pp. 342–43.
305. Ibid., pp. 21–23.
306. John Knox, *History of Morgan County,* pp. 84–85.
307. John Knox, "Wooley's Springs—A Limestone 'First,' Limestone Creek Was Named By Early Settlers," *Decatur Daily,* September 30, 1964.
308. Ibid.
309. "Historic Sites," XV (1953), p. 366; Owen, II, p. 1295.

BIBLIOGRAPHY

BOOKS AND MANUSCRIPTS

Abernethy, Thomas Perkins. *The Formative Period in Alabama, 1815–1828.* Montgomery, 1922.

Adair, James. *The History of the American Indians.* London, 1775.

Armes, Ethel. *The Story of Coal and Iron in Alabama.* Birmingham, 1910.

Ball, Rev. T. H. *A Glance Into The Great South-East, or, Clarke County, Alabama, And Its Surroundings, From 1540 to 1877.* Grove Hill, 1882.

Berney, Saffold. *Hand Book of Alabama: A Complete Index to the State.* Mobile, 1878.

Betts, Edward Chambers. *Early History of Huntsville, Alabama, 1804 to 1870.* Montgomery, 1916.

Blackford, Randolph F. *Fascinating Talladega County: Rich in History and in Legends.* Talladega, n.d.

Blue, M. P. *City Directory and History of Montgomery, Alabama.* Montgomery, 1878.

Bourne, Edward Gaylord, ed. *Narratives of the Career of Hernando de Soto.* New York, 1904.

Brewer, Willis. *Alabama: Her History, Resources, War Record, and Public Men.* Montgomery, 1872.

Brown, John P. *Old Frontiers: The Story of the Cherokee Indians From Earliest Times to the Date of Their Removal to the West, 1838.* Kingsport, 1938.

Carter, Clarence Edwin, ed. *The Territorial Papers of the United States.* XVIII. Washington, 1952.

Caughey, John Walton. *McGillivray of the Creeks.* Norman, 1938.

Claiborne, John Francis Hamtramck. *Life and Times of General Sam. Dale, The Mississippi Partisan.* New York, 1860.

Clinton, Matthew William. *Tuscaloosa, Alabama: Its Early Days, 1816–1865.* Tuscaloosa, 1958.

Comings, L. J. Newcomb and Albers, Martha M. *A Brief History of Baldwin County.* Fairhope, 1928.

Delaney, Caldwell. *The Story of Mobile.* Mobile, 1953.

Dow, Lorenzo. *The Dealings of God, Man, And The Devil; As Exemplified In The Life, Experience, And Travels of Lorenzo Dow, In a Period Of Over Half A Century.* St. Louis, 1850.

Elliott, Carl, ed. *Annals Of Northwest Alabama.* 4 vols. Tuscaloosa, 1958.

Ellison, Rhoda Coleman. *History and Bibliography of Alabama Newspapers in the Nineteenth Century.* University, 1954.

Fleming, Walter L. *Civil War and Reconstruction in Alabama.* New York, 1905.

Foster, Henry B. *History of the Tuscaloosa County Baptist Association, 1834–1934.* Tuscaloosa, 1934.

Frazer, Mell A. *Early History of Steamboats In Alabama.* Auburn, 1907.

Fry, Anna M. Gayle. *Memories Of Old Cahaba.* n.p., 1905.

Garrett, William. *Reminiscences of Public Men In Alabama, For Thirty Years.* Atlanta, 1872.

Gatschet, Albert Samuel. *A Migration Legend of the Creek Indians, With a Linguistic, Historic, and Ethnolographic Introduction.* 2 vols. Philadelphia, 1884–1888.

Halbert, H. S. and Ball, T. H. *The Creek War of 1813 and 1814.* Chicago, 1895. Reprinted by The University of Alabama Press, 1969.

Hamilton, Peter J. *Colonial Mobile: An Historical Study.* Boston, 1897. Reprinted by The University of Alabama Press, 1976.

Hammond, Ralph. *Ante-Bellum Mansions of Alabama.* New York, 1951.

Hardy, John. *Selma: Her Institutions and Her Men.* Selma, 1879.

Harris, W. Stuart. *Southern Historical Records.* 50 vols. Unpublished manuscripts, 1960–1976.

———. *A Short History of Marion, Perry County, Alabama: Its Homes and Its Buildings.* Marion, 1970.

———. *Diaries of American History, 1492–1865, For Use in Secondary School Social Studies.* Unpublished dissertation, University of Alabama, 1970.

———. *Diaries of the American Frontier.* Unpublished manuscript, 1967.

———. *Early American Diaries, 1492–1781.* Unpublished manuscript, 1968.

Hawkins, Benjamin. *A Sketch of the Creek Country 1798–1799.* Savannah, 1848.

Henry, Robert Selph, ed. *As They Saw Forrest.* Jackson, 1956.

Holt, Thad. *Old Gainesville, 1832–1875.* Birmingham, 1955.

Hoole, W. Stanley. *Alias Simon Suggs, The Life and Times of Johnson Jones Hooper.* University of Alabama, 1952.

Hurtel, Caroline Gaillard. *The River Plantation of Thomas and Marianne Gaillard, 1832–1850.* Mobile, 1959.

Jackson, Walter M. *The Story of Selma.* Birmingham, 1954.

Jemison, E. Grace. *Historic Tales of Talladega, Prior to the Twentieth Century.* Montgomery, 1959.

Johnson, Robert Underwood and Clough, Clarence, eds. *Battles and Leaders of the Civil War.* 4 vols. New York, 1956.

Jones, Charles G. *The Dead Towns of Georgia.* Savannah, 1878.

―――. *History of Georgia.* Savannah, 1883.

Knox, John. *A History of Morgan County, Alabama.* Decatur, 1966.

Leftwich, Nina. *Two Hundred Years At Muscle Shoals.* Birmingham, 1935.

Lewis, B. Palmer. *John Hardie of Thornhill, His Life, Letters and Times.* New York, 1928.

Little, John Buckner. *The History of Butler County, Alabama, From 1815 to 1885.* Cincinnati, 1885.

McClellan, Captain R. A. *Early History of Limestone County.* Athens, 1881.

McKenney, Thomas L. and Hall, James. *History of the Indian Tribes of North America.* Philadelphia, 1844. Reprinted and edited by James D. Horan as *The McKenney-Hall Portrait Gallery of American Indians.* New York, 1972.

McMillan, Malcolm C. *Yesterday's Birmingham.* Miami, 1975.

Marengo County Board of Revenue. *Dedication: Marengo County Courthouse 1968 A.D.* n.p., n.d.

Maxwell, James Robert. *Autobiography of James Robert Maxwell.* New York, 1926.

Moore, Albert Burton. *History of Alabama.* Tuscaloosa, 1951.

Neville, Bert. *A Glance At Old Cahawba, Alabama's Early Capital.* Selma, 1961.

―――. *Directory of River Packets in the Mobile-Alabama-Warrior-Tombigbee Trades, 1818–1932.* Selma, 1962.

Owen, Marie Bankhead. *The Story of Alabama: A History of the State.* 5 vols. New York, 1949.

Owen, Thomas McAdory. *History of Alabama and Dictionary of Alabama Biography.* 4 vols. Chicago, 1921.

Pickett, Albert James. *History of Alabama and Incidentally of Georgia and Mississippi, From the Earliest Period.* Charleston, 1851. This work was reprinted in one volume by the Birmingham Book and Magazine Co. in 1962.

Pioneers Club. *Early Days in Birmingham.* Birmingham, 1937.

Riley, Benjamin Franklin. *History of Conecuh County, Alabama.* Columbus, 1881.

Robbins, Maurice. *The Amateur Archaeologist's Handbook.* New York, 1965.

Royall, Anne Newport. *Letters From Alabama 1817–1822.* Washington, 1830.

Saunders, James Edmonds. *Early Settlers of Alabama.* New Orleans, 1899.

Schoolcraft, Henry Rowe. *History of the Indian Tribes of the United States: Their Present Conditions and Prospects, and a Sketch of Their Ancient Status.* Philadelphia, 1857.

Selma and Dallas County Sesquicentennial Committee. *150 Years, Selma and Dallas County.* Selma, 1969.

Smith, Nelson F. *History of Pickens County, Alabama, From Its First Settlement.* Carrollton, 1856.

Smith, William R., Sr. *Reminiscences of a Long Life; Historical, Political, Personal and Literary.* Washington, 1889.

Snedecor, V. Gayle. *A Directory of Greene County For 1855–56.* Mobile, 1856.

Sulzby, James F., Jr. *Historic Alabama Hotels and Resorts.* University of Alabama, 1960.

———. *Birmingham, As It Was, in Jackson County.* Birmingham, 1944.

Swanton, John R. *The Indian Tribes of North America.* Washington, 1971.

Townes, S. A. *The History of Marion: Sketches of Life in Perry County, Alabama.* Marion, 1844.

Walker, Anne Kendrick. *Backtracking in Barbour County: A Narrative of the Last Alabama Frontier.* Richmond, 1941.

West, Anson. *History of Methodism in Alabama.* Nashville, 1893.

Woodward, Thomas S. *Woodward's Reminiscences of the Creek, or Muscogee Indians, Contained in Letters to Friends in Georgia and Alabama.* Montgomery, 1859.

Work Projects Administration. *Alabama: A Guide to the Deep South.* New York, 1941.

Wyeth, John Allen. *That Devil Forrest: Life of General Nathan Bedford Forrest.* New York, 1959.

Yerby, William Edward Wadsworth. *History of Greensboro, Alabama From Its Earliest Settlement.* Montgomery, 1908.

Articles and Periodicals

Adams, George I. "A Century of Gold Mining in Alabama," *Alabama Historical Quarterly,* I (Fall, 1930), pp. 271–79.

Andrews, Daniel Marshall. "DeSoto's Route From Cofitachequi, in Georgia, to Cosa, in Alabama," in Marie Bankhead Owen, *The Story of Alabama,* I, pp. 122–29.

Andrews, W. L. "Early History of Southeast Alabama," *Alabama Historical Quarterly*, X (1948), 99–132.

Brannon, Peter A. "The Route of DeSoto From Cosa to Mauvilla," in Marie Bankhead Owen, *The Story of Alabama*, I, pp. 189–90.

––––––. "The Cahawba Military Prison, 1863–1865," *Alabama Review*, III (July, 1950), pp. 163–73.

––––––. "Indian Treaties," *Alabama Historical Quarterly*, XII (1950), pp. 242–50.

––––––. "Old Glennville: An Early Center of East Alabama Culture," *Alabama Review*, XI (October, 1958), pp. 255–66.

––––––. "Russell County," *Alabama Historical Quarterly*, XXI (1959), pp. 1–122.

Brewer, George Evans. "History of Coosa County," *Alabama Historical Quarterly*, IV (Spring, 1942), pp. 1–151; IV (Summer, 1942), pp. 157–285.

Cargile, John. "In Winston County Tiny, Run-down Jail Symbolizes Bloody Era," *Birmingham News*, August 17, 1969.

Chambers, Nella Jean. "The Creek Indian Factory at Fort Mitchell," *Alabama Historical Quarterly*, XXI (1959), pp. 15–53.

––––––. "Early Days In East Alabama," *Alabama Review*, XIII (July, 1960), pp. 177–84.

Cobbs, Hamner. "Geography of the Vine and Olive Colony," *Alabama Review*, XIV (April, 1961), pp. 83–97.

Collins, William B. "The Crawford-Burnside Duel," *Gulf States Historical Magazine*, II (July, 1903), p. 54.

Cook, Ford. "Scenes Of Century Ago Visualized From Trace Of Baldwin Settlement," *Mobile Press Register*, January 22, 1961.

Corcoran, Larry. "Piper: Mere Ghost Town," *Birmingham News*, June 23, 1967.

Covington, Stuart. "Memphis On Tombigbee—Once Thriving Port Now Gone," *Birmingham News*, July 31, 1960.

Crenshaw, Rev. E. C. "Indian Massacres in Butler County in 1818," Alabama Historical Society, *Transactions*, IV (1899–1903), pp. 99–102.

Deer, Elizabeth S., ed. "Torrey-Dellet Correspondence, 1843–1845," *Alabama Historical Quarterly*, XIX (Summer, 1957), pp. 304–51.

Doster, James F., ed. "Letters Relating to the Tragedy of Fort Mims: August–September, 1813," *Alabama Review*, XIV (October, 1961), pp. 269–91.

DuBose, Euba Eugenia. "The History of Mount Sterling," *Alabama Historical Quarterly*, XXV (Fall, 1963), pp. 297–369.

DuBose, John Witherspoon. "Chronicles of the Canebrake, 1817–1860," *Alabama Historical Quarterly*, IX (Winter, 1947), pp. 475–613.

Emerson, O. B. "The Bonapartist Exiles in Alabama," *Alabama Review*, XI (April, 1958), pp. 135–43.

Farmer, Margaret Pace. "Early History of Pike County, Alabama," *Alabama Historical Quarterly*, X (1948), pp. 26–50.

Foreman, Carolyn Thomas. "John Gunter and His Family," *Alabama Historical Quarterly*, IX (Fall, 1947), pp. 412–51.

Foshee, John H. "Alabama's Forgotten Battles: Fort Blakely and Spanish Fort," *Birmingham News Magazine*, December 5, 1965.

Fosque, Virginia Oden. "Sumter County Place-Names: A Selection," *Alabama Review*, XIII (January, 1960), 52–67.

Gaines, George S. "Gaines' Reminiscences," *Alabama Historical Quarterly*, XXVI (Fall & Winter, 1964), pp. 133–230.

Griffith, Lucille. "South Carolina and Fort Alabama, 1714–1763," *Alabama Review*, XII (October, 1959), 258–71.

Guinn, J. M. K. "History of Randolph County," *Alabama Historical Quarterly*, IV (Fall, 1942), pp. 291–413.

Hamilton, Peter J. "Early Roads of Alabama," Alabama Historical Society, *Transactions*, II (1897–98), pp. 39–56.

———— and Owen, Thomas McAdory. "Topographical Notes and Observations On The Alabama River, August, 1814. By Major Howell Tatum," Alabama Historical Society, *Transactions*, II (1897–98), pp. 130–77.

Hardy, John. "History of Autauga County," *Daily State Sentinel*, August 10, 1867, reprinted in *Alabama Historical Quarterly*, III (Spring, 1941), 96–116.

Hill, Thomas F. "Independence, Ala.: Town Quite Busy Going Nowhere," *Birmingham News*, July 2, 1963.

Holmes, Jack D. L. "Fort Stoddart in 1799: Seven Letters of Captain Bartholomew Schaumburgh," *Alabama Historical Quarterly*, XXVI (Fall, 1964), 231–52.

————. "Notes On The Spanish Fort San Esteban De Tombecbe," *Alabama Review*, XVIII (October, 1965), pp. 281–90.

Hoole, W. Stanley, ed. "Elyton, Alabama, and The Connecticut Asylum: The Letters of William H. Ely, 1820–1821," *Alabama Review*, III (January, 1950), pp. 36–69.

Howard, Milo B., ed. "Governor John Gill Shorter Executive Papers," *Alabama Historical Quarterly*, XXIII (Fall, 1961), pp. 278–84.

Irons, George. "River Ferries in Alabama Before 1861," *Alabama Review*, IV (January, 1951), pp. 22–37.

Ivey, Betty Dickinson. "From River To Rail In Pickens County," *Alabama Review*, VII (January, 1954), pp. 53–66.

James, R. L. "Colbertians," *Alabama Historical Quarterly*, VII (Summer, 1945), pp. 159–222.

Jenkins, William H. "Alabama Forts, 1700–1838," *Alabama Review*, XII (July, 1959), pp. 163–80.

———. "Some Alabama Dead Towns," *Alabama Review*, XII (October, 1959), pp. 281–85.

King, H. M. "Historical Sketches of Macon County," *Alabama Historical Quarterly*, XVIII (Summer, 1956), pp. 187–217.

Knox, John. " 'Countrymen' Tied Pioneers To Indians, Helped Change the Face of the Frontier," *Decatur Daily*, November 29, 1954.

———. "Roses Reveal Site of the Lost Academy, LaGrange Was An Active And Bustling Town," *Decatur Daily*, November 15, 1964.

———. "Wooley's Springs—A Limestone 'First', Limestone Creek Was Named By Early Settlers," *Decatur Daily*, September 30, 1964.

Krouse, T. J. "Clarke County Salt Works," *Alabama Historical Quarterly*, XX (Spring, 1958), pp. 95–100.

Langley, J. T. "Alabama's Gold Rush Was A Real Lulu," *Birmingham News Magazine*, May 5, 1963.

McGroarty, William Buckner. "Diary of Captain William Buckner," *William and Mary Quarterly*, VI (July, 1926), pp. 173–207.

Malone, Thomas Smith. "Scraps Relating To The Early History of Limestone County," *Alabama Historical Quarterly*, XVIII (Fall, 1956), pp. 309–80.

Marks, Laurence H. "Fort Mims: A Challenge," *Alabama Review*, XVIII (October, 1965), pp. 275–80.

Massey, W. M. "Legendary Falls Will Drown In Own Water," *Birmingham News Magazine*, February 12, 1961.

Mims, Shadrack. "History of Autauga County," *Alabama Historical Quarterly*, VIII (Fall, 1946), pp. 241–68.

Owen, Thomas McAdory. "Indian Tribes and Towns in Alabama," *Alabama Historical Quarterly*, XII (1950), pp. 118–241.

———. "Notes on Alabama Mounds and Antiquities," Alabama Historical Society, *Transactions*, IV (1899–1903), pp. 235–44.

Palmer, Edward. "Alabama Notes Made in 1883–84," *Alabama Historical Quarterly*, XXII (Winter, 1960), 244–72.

Pearson, Theodore Bowling. "Early Settlement Around Historic McIntosh Bluff: Alabama's First County Seat," *Alabama Review*, XXIII (October, 1970), pp. 243–55.

Penicaut, M. "Annals of Louisiana, From 1698 to 1722," *Alabama Historical Quarterly*, V (Fall, 1943), pp. 261–355.

Phelps, Dawson A. "The Natchez Trace In Albaama," *Alabama Review*, VII (January, 1954), pp. 22–41.

———. "Colbert Ferry and Selected Documents," *Alabama Historical Quarterly*, XXV (Fall, 1963), pp. 203–26.

Plaisance, Father Aloysius. "The Choctaw Trading House, 1803–

1822," *Alabama Historical Quarterly*, XVI (Fall & Winter, 1954), pp. 393–423.

Rea, Robert R. "The Trouble At Tombeckby," *Alabama Review*, XXI (January, 1968), pp. 21–39.

Richards, E. G. "Reminiscences of the Early Days in Chambers County," *Alabama Historical Quarterly*, IV (Fall, 1942), pp. 417–45.

Russell, Robert A. "Gold Mining in Alabama Before 1860," *Alabama Review*, X (January, 1957), pp. 5–14.

Scribner, Robert Leslie. "A Short History of Brewton, Alabama," *Alabama Historical Quarterly*, XI (1949), pp.1–131.

Sikora, Frank. "When Mines Close Few Folks Stay in Empty Towns," *Birmingham News*, February 16, 1969.

Smith, Winston. "Early History of Demopolis," *Alabama Review*, XVIII (April, 1965), pp. 83–91.

Sparrow, Hugh W. "Once Busy State Capital: Rivers, Rerouting Railroads Reduce Cahaba to Ghost Town," *Birmingham News*, July 17, 1960.

Street, Oliver Day. "The Indians of Marshall County, Alabama," Alabama Historical Society, *Transactions*, IV (1899–1903), pp. 193–210.

Thomas, Daniel H. "Fort Toulouse: The French Outpost at the Alibamos on the Coosa," *Alabama Historical Quarterly*, XXII (Fall, 1960), pp. 141–230.

Wallace, Walker D. "Old Hickory Camped Here," *Birmingham News Magazine*, August 14, 1960.

Watson, Elbert L. "Gadsden From Tepees To Steamboats," *Alabama Review*, XI (October, 1958), pp. 243–54.

Welsh, Mary. "Reminiscences of Old Saint Stephens, of More Than Sixty-five Years Ago," Alabama Historical Society, *Transactions*, III (1898–99), pp. 208–26.

Whitfield, Gaius, Jr. "The French Grant in Alabama, A History of the Founding of Demopolis," Alabama Historical Society, *Transactions*, IV (1899–1903), pp. 231–55.

Wyman, William Stokes. "Early Times in the Vicinity of the Present City of Montgomery," Alabama Historical Society, *Transactions*, II (1897–1898), pp. 28–33.

MAPS (IN CHRONOLOGICAL ORDER)

"Original Map of the Explorations of Soto and Moscoso, 1539–1543." The Alabama Archaeological Society, *Stones and Bones: Projectile Point Primer*. Birmingham, n.d. p. 4.

"Florida et Apalche," 1597. The original is in the Spanish Archives; copy in John P. Brown, *Old Frontiers, The Story of the Cherokee Indians From Earliest Times to the Date of Their Removal to the West.* Kingsport, 1938. p. 34.

"The Southeastern Part of the Present United States From the Popple Map of 1733." The Alabama Archaeological Society, *Stones and Bones: Projectile Point Primer.* Birmingham, n.d. p. 3.

"Map of the Town of Cahawba." Alabama Department of Archives and History, Montgomery.

"Map of Hickory Ground or Little Tallassee." *Arrow Points,* XIV (Winter, 1913), p. 48.

"Map of Tukabahchi." *Arrow Points,* XIV (Fall, 1913), p. 35.

Copies of the following maps were found in Peter J. Hamilton, *Colonial Mobile: A Study of Southwestern History.* Mobile, 1952:

"Fort Louis de la Mobille, 1702," p. 52.

"New Fort Louis, 1711," p. 86.

"Danville's Map of Mobile Bay and Coast, about 1732," p. 166.

"Danville's Map of the River Basin, about 1732," p. 188.

"De Crenay's Map, 1733," p. 190.

"Bowen's Map of the Indian Nations in British Times, 1764," p. 240.

"British Admiralty Chart of Mobile Bay and Coast, 1771," p. 260.

The following maps were found in the Special Collections Department, University of Alabama Library:

"Reid's American Atlas," 1796.

"Map of the Mississippi Territory," 1804.

"A List of All the Houses on the River Tombekby and River Tansaw [*sic*]," 1804.

"Map of the Late Surveys in the Northern District of the Alabama Territory," by Peel E. Sannoner, 1817.

"Map of Alabama, Constructed From the Surveys in the General Land Office and Other Documents," by John Melish, 1818.

"Early's Map of Georgia," 1818, showing the Creek Nation.

"Geographical, Statistical, and Historical Map of Alabama," by E. Lucas, Jr., 1819.

"Map of Alabama," by E. Lucas, Jr., 1822.

"Map of Alabama," by A. Finley, 1830.

"The Travellers Pocket Map of Alabama with its Roads & Distances from place to place, along the Stage & Steam Boat Routes," by H. S. Tanner, 1830.

"A New Map of Alabama with its Roads & Distances from place to place, along the Stage & Steam Boat Routes," by H. S. Tanner, 1836.

"Map of Alabama," by T. G. Bradford, 1838.

"Map of Alabama," by H. S. Tanner, 1839.

"Map of the State of Alabama," by J. Greenleaf, 1842.

"Map of Alabama," by Sidney E. Morse and Samuel Breese, 1842.

"A New Map of Alabama with its Roads & Distances from place to place, along the Stage & Steam Boat Routes," by H. N. Burroughs, 1846.

"A New Map of Alabama with its Roads & Distances from place to place, along the Stage & Steam Boat Routes," by Thomas Cowperthwait & Co., 1850.

"Map of Alabama," by J. H. Colton & Co., 1853.

"Map of Alabama," by A. & C. Black, Edinburgh, 1856.

"Colton's Alabama," 1859.

"Southern Mississippi & Alabama, Showing the Approaches to Mobile," Coast Survey Office, 1863.

"Gray's Atlas Map of Alabama," 1874.

"Colton's Alabama," 1878.

"Cram's Railroad & Township Map of Alabama," 1879.

"Alabama Map," 1904.

Also used in this study were maps obtained from the U.S. Geological Survey and various county maps from the Alabama State Highway Department, which are too numerous to list.

A LISTING OF DEAD
TOWNS BY COUNTIES

Sites of dead towns are found in every county in Alabama, but the author of this volume has found no towns of the historic era in Crenshaw, Geneva, Lamar, or Pike counties. Each of these four counties contains the remains of ancient, unnamed Indian towns and villages. Though remains of aboriginal villages are not numerous in Crenshaw County, several sites do exist in the vicinity of Glenwood Station, including two large and one small mound 2 miles northwest of this small community. In Geneva County, sites are found on the Choctawhatchee River near Pate's Landing. Although embracing lands formerly held by the Chickasaws, Lamar County was only used as a hunting ground. There are several mounds in Pike County, including those located on Beeman's Creek, 9 miles northwest of Troy, containing four burial mounds which have been almost destroyed in modern times. There are also three mounds on Indian Creek, 12 miles west of Troy.

Dead towns included in this volume, indexed according to the counties in which they are located are:

AUTAUGA COUNTY: Autauga 3; Independence 85; Kingston 88; Vernon 108; Washington 109
BALDWIN COUNTY: Alabama City 58; Blakeley 63; Fort Blakeley 37; Fort Mims 45; Fort Montgomery 46; Fort Pierce 47; Honey Cut 84; Navy Cove 94; Rocky Hill 101; Spanish Fort 50; Village 109; Williamsburg 111
BARBOUR COUNTY: Tamali 29; Williamston 111
BIBB COUNTY: Bibb Court House 62; Piper 98
BLOUNT COUNTY: Hanbyville 83; Little Warrior 90

BULLOCK COUNTY: Chananagi 6
BUTLER COUNTY: Fort Bibb 36; Fort Dale 40, 79; Middleton 93
CALHOUN COUNTY: Fort Chinnabee 38; Talishatchie 28
CHAMBERS COUNTY: Chambers Court House 70; Fort Tyler 55
CHEROKEE COUNTY: Fort Armstrong 35; Goshen 82; Turkey
  Town 31
CHILTON COUNTY: Pakan Talahassi 25
CHOCTAW COUNTY: Ashford Springs 60; Bladon Springs 62; Cato's
  Fort 38; Fakitchipunta 10
CLARKE COUNTY: Clarkesville 72; Curry's Fort 40; Fakitchipunta
  10; Fort Carney 38; Fort Easley 41; Fort Gullett 41; Fort Lavier 43;
  Fort Madison 44; Fort Sinquefield 49; Fort White 55; Glass Redoubt
  41; Landrum's Fort 42; McGrew's Fort 44; Turner's Fort 54
CLAY COUNTY: Anatitchapko 2; Hillabi 11; Imukfa 13; Wako Kayi 32
CLEBURNE COUNTY: Arbacoochee 59; Chulafinnee 71
COFFEE COUNTY: Brunson 66; Wellborn 110
COLBERT COUNTY: Colbert's Ferry 73; Doublehead's Village 9; New
  York 96; Oka Kapassa 22; South Port 104
CONECUH COUNTY: Hampton Ridge 82; Sparta 105
COOSA COUNTY: Lalokalka 15; Lexington 89; Okchayi 23; Opil´ako
  24; Pakan Talahassi 25; Weogufki 32
COVINGTON COUNTY: Montezuma 94
CRENSHAW COUNTY: see 145
CULLMAN COUNTY: Fall Creek 78
DALE COUNTY: Richmond 101
DALLAS COUNTY: Cahaba 66; Casiste 6; Humati 12; Kaxa 14; Red
  Bluff 99; Talisi 28
DE KALB COUNTY: Bootsville 65; Rawlingsville 99; Will's Town 32
ELMORE COUNTY: Fort Jackson 42; Fort Toulouse 54; Fusi-Hatchi
  10; Hatchitchapa 10; Hoithlewalli 11; Kailaidshi 13; Koasati 14;
  Kulumi 15; Odshiapofa 22; Okchayudshi 23; Pakana 24; Taskigi 29;
  Tomonpa 30; Tukabatchi 31; Weemooka 32
ESCAMBIA COUNTY: Fillmore 79; Fort Crawford 39
ETOWAH COUNTY: Bennettsville 61
FAYETTE COUNTY: New River 95
FRANKLIN COUNTY: Burleson 66; LaGrange 88; New Boston 94
GENEVA COUNTY: see 145
GREENE COUNTY: Cabusto 6; Springfield 106
HALE COUNTY: Candy's Landing 68; Erie 77; Hollow Square 84;
  Piachi 25
HENRY COUNTY: Chiska Talofa 7; Franklin 80

HOUSTON COUNTY: Yufali 33

JACKSON COUNTY: Bellefonte 61; Birmingham 62; Chiaha 6; Crowtown 9; Larkin's Fork 89; Sauta 26

JEFFERSON COUNTY: Carrollsville 69; Elyton 75; Hanbyville 83; Jonesboro 87

LAMAR COUNTY: see 145

LAUDERDALE COUNTY: Bainbridge 60

LAWRENCE COUNTY: Gumpond 82; Melton's Bluff 92

LEE COUNTY: Witumka 33

LIMESTONE COUNTY: Bridgewater 65; Cambridge 68; Cotton Port 74; Fort Hampton 41; Sulphur Branch Trestle Fort 52; Wooley's Springs 112

LOWNDES COUNTY: Fort Deposit 40; Ikanatchaka 12

MACON COUNTY: Autossee 4; Fort Bainbridge 36; Fort Decatur 40; Fort Hull 42; Old Talisi 28; Thloblocco 30; Yufali 33

MADISON COUNTY: Ditto's Landing 74; Triana 107

MARENGO COUNTY: Aigleville 57; Arcola 60; New Boston 95

MARION COUNTY: Pikeville 97

MARSHALL COUNTY: Claysville 73; Coste 8; Creek Path 8; Fort Deposit 40; Gunter's Village 10; Tali 27

MOBILE COUNTY: Fort Condé 39; Fort Louis de la Mobile 43; Fort Powell 48; Fort Stoddert 51; Mount Vernon Cantonment and Arsenal 46; Portersville 98

MONROE COUNTY: Claiborne 71; Fort Claiborne 38; Piachi 25

MONTGOMERY COUNTY: Ecunchati 9; Muklasa 20; Sawanogi 26; Tawasa 30

MORGAN COUNTY: Bluff City 65; Centreville 69; Fall Creek 78; Stringer 106; Sunnyside 107; Valhermoso Springs 108; Winton 111

PERRY COUNTY: Athahatchee 3; Cahaba Old Town 67

PICKENS COUNTY: Fairfield 78; Memphis 93; Vienna 109

PIKE COUNTY: see 145

RANDOLPH COUNTY: Atchinalgi 3; Louina 90

RUSSELL COUNTY: Apalatchukla 3; Fort Bainbridge 36; Fort Mitchell 46; Glennville 80; Kawita Talahassi 13; Okoni 24; Osotchi 24; Sand Fort 49; Sawokli 26

ST. CLAIR COUNTY: Fort Strother 52; Littafuchee 16

SHELBY COUNTY: Shelby Springs 103; Shelbyville 104

SUMTER COUNTY: Bodka Village 5; Fort Tombécbee 53; Jamestown 86; Quilby 25

TALLADEGA COUNTY: Abihka 1; Abikudshi 1; Chalakagay 6; Chandler Springs 70; Chickasaw Town 7; Coosa 7; Fort Lashley 43; Fort

Williams 55; Ironaton 85; Jenifer 86; Mardisville 91; Nauche 21; Nottingham 96; Renfroe 100; Talatigi 27; Talinachusy 27; Tasqui 29; Yufaula 33

TALLAPOOSA COUNTY: Cholocco Litabixee 7; Dudleyville 74; Goldville 81; Hillabi 11; Niuyaka 21; Old Talisi 28; Suka-Ispoka 26; Young's Ferry 112

TUSCALOOSA COUNTY: Black Warrior's Town 4; Newtown 95; Oregonia 97

WALKER COUNTY: America 59; Black Warrior's Town 4

WASHINGTON COUNTY: Cato's Fort 38; Dumfries 75; Fort St. Stephens 48; McIntosh Bluff 90; St. Stephens 101; Wakefield 109

WILCOX COUNTY: Canton Bluff 69; Humati 12; Nanipacna 20; Prairie Bluff 98; Rehoboth 100; Upper Peach Tree 107; Uxapita 32

WINSTON COUNTY: Falls City 78; Gumpond 82; Houston 84; New London 95; Thornhill 107

INDEX

Williams, Colonel, 56
Williams, Fort, 55–56
Williams' Settlement, 111
Williamston, 111
Will's Town, 32–33
Wilson, James H., 76
Wilson's Raiders, 55, 83–84
Winn, Camp, 104
Winston, John A., 6
Winton, 111–12

Winton, George, 112
Witumka, 33
Wi-wux-ka, 32
Wolf King, 20
Womack, Jesse, 79
Wood, W.B., 85
Woodward, Thomas, 33
Wooley, Joel, 112
Wooley's Springs, 112
Woolfolk, General, 46

York Bluff, 96
York, Fort, 53
Youngs, White, 40
Young's Ferry, 112
Yufala, 33
Yufalahatchi, 33
Yufali, 33–34
Yufaula, 33

Zabusta, 6